THE FAIRTRY E:

John E. (Jack) Campbell joined the ~~~~~~~~~ ~~press in Glasgow as a 15 year old copy boy, and a year later, as its first cub reporter, he began a long and distinguished career in journalism. When the war began he was deputy chief sub editor. He joined the Navy's deep sea rescue tugs section and served almost six years, mostly in the Atlantic, latterly in command of one of the vessels.

Demobilised as Lieutenant RNR, he rejoined the *Express* where he occupied various executive posts, including editorship of the *Evening Citizen* and of the *Scottish Sunday Express*. After retiring from the *Express*, he continued as a freelance, mainly editing company newspapers and magazines. The first of these was Salvesen's *Salvo*.

At Salvesen's headquarters he was intrigued to find a solitary fishing vessel among the models and pictures of the merchant and whaling fleets, and he decided to find out more about this stranger in the tribe. . . .

To James.

THE FAIRTRY EXPERIMENT

JACK CAMPBELL

You can read of the reasons why I was away from home on so many occasions when you were only a little boy in the 40's and 50's.

Best wishes,

Dad,

29th June 1995.

EDINBURGH
B&W PUBLISHING
1995

First published 1995
by B&W Publishing
Edinburgh

Copyright © Jack Campbell 1995

ISBN 1 873631 57 X

British Library Cataloguing in Publication Data:
A catalogue record for this book is available from
the British Library

Cover design: Harry Palmer

Printed by WSOY

PREFACE

A fishing vessel unlike any other appeared in the River Humber in the 1950s.

This was *Fairtry*, the first stern-trawling factory ship.

The idea of such a vessel began with Sir Charles Dennistoun Burney, a prolific inventor who had never engaged in the fishing industry but who believed that he could change the face of it.

The concept was given reality thereafter by Captain Harold Keith Salvesen, head of what was then the largest individual whaling concern in the world, who had never engaged in the fishing industry either but was prepared to gamble that the inventor was right.

When *Fairtry* first sailed out of the Humber the dispute with Iceland that was the prelude to the 'Cod Wars' was a mere skirmish of words; the 200 mile limit that was destined to destroy the great British distant water fleet was seen as little more than an absurdity; every vessel trawled from the side, and for nearly every trawler owner to freeze at sea was an exercise in futility, yet on shore a frozen foods industry was developing which is huge business today.

Captain Harold Salvesen built *Fairtry* because he foresaw that inadequate conservation of the whale was leading to its extinction and to the demise of whaling, and he thought that in deep sea fishing he might find an alternative activity.

His venture revolutionised deep sea fishing. Every major catching nation built in *Fairtry*'s image, and over two decades they opened up vast areas of oceans that had been barely exploited.

Fairtry took Captain Harold's company out of whaling. But she led along a path very different from the one he envisaged.

Many people gave encouragement and help during the search to piece together the strands of her story. They are too numerous to list, but thanks are due in particular to the following:–

Christian Salvesen PLC, which gave unrestricted access to minutes and memoranda and freedom to talk at length with its principals and staff.

Mr William Lochridge, aide and friend of the inventor, Sir Charles Dennistoun Burney.

Sir Cecil Burney, son of the inventor.

The late Dr. W. J. Lyon Dean, OBE, for many years a member of the White Fish Authority and chairman of the Herring Industry Board.

Dr. J. J. Connell, CBE, director (retired) of Torry Research Station, and its staff.

Mr Neil B. McKellar, chief economist, the Sea Fish Industry Authority.

Mr Kenneth Beeken, secretary of the Grimsby Fish Merchants Association Ltd.

The friendly and patient staff of Grimsby Central Library.

The assistance of all others is acknowledged with sincere gratitude although they are not named individually.

CHAPTER ONE

You could tell at a glance that at one time she must have cut a quite dashing figure.

Her Greek owner, Mr Costas Keletchekis, head of the K.M. Corporation of Panama, had acquired her 13 years before when she wore the Red Duster.

But *Joy 2*, mother ship to a fleet of shrimp catchers in the Persian Gulf, was now 31 years old, toilworn and showing her age, and Mr Keletchekis decided she would have to go. He sent her to the scrapyard.

For ten years her name had not appeared in Lloyd's Register of Shipping. The last entry, in 1974/5, said her surveys were overdue, her class suspended.

She is worthy of a different epitaph.

Her original name was *Fairtry*.

Although she was launched into the River Dee at Aberdeen in 1953, we have to begin her story in the closing years of the war, in the little seaside town of Saltcoats on the Firth of Clyde, where the second baronet Burney, who preferred to be known as Sir Dennis rather than by his Christian names of Charles Dennistoun, was lodging in a boarding house owned by two old ladies. The house was conveniently close to the ICI explosives factory at Ardeer, in a secluded workshop of which he was developing in secret a range of new recoilless guns and special projectiles with which to confront the enemy.

The smallest of these was a 3.45 inch gun, with a projectile similar in size to an orthodox artillery 25 pounder, but able to be fired in the same way as a rifle while balanced on a man's shoulder.

He had developed the theory of the shoulder gun in the garage of his home at Maynard's Park in Cranleigh, Surrey, with an old elephant hunting gun which he adapted and fitted with a long bell-mouthed tube like the exhaust of a motorcycle engine, this to balance the blast rather than the butt of the gun taking recoil.

At the other end of the range was an 8 inch gun designed to be able to fire a shell for 20 miles, with double the explosive charge of a 12 inch naval gun.

Occasionally he went back to Maynard's Park, where Lady Burney had continued to stay, and occasionally he saw his only son Cecil when that young man had leave from the Navy. But the last time he had gone to their London home in Carlton Park Terrace a presentiment had caused him to go out, and he returned to find that a German bomb had left only a gaping hole.

At 55 years of age, he was partly bald, compactly built, in manner direct and decisive, but withal quiet and deliberate. The absence of flamboyancy was in inverse proportion to the rash of newspaper headlines in which he had figured throughout his career.

As 16 year old Midshipman Dennis Burney he had followed a family naval tradition which could trace back to an Admiral Burney who served with Nelson. Early in his naval career he borrowed a primitive aeroplane to locate a sunken submarine and was inspired by this to study aeronautics. Convinced that planes should be used to attack submarines, when he was 23 years old he built a seaplane for which the Admiralty gave facilities for trials 'at Lieutenant Burney's expense'. In August 1912 it was enough of a novelty to cause crowds to follow its progress as he and a companion test-flew it along England's south coast.

His father Cecil, the first baronet, was Jellicoe's second in command at the battle of Jutland, and latterly Second Sea Lord. But the Kaiser war brought as much fame to the son. A picture on the front page of the now-defunct *Daily Sketch* portrayed him riding in a carriage with his father. A headline above it said 'Mastered Hun Submarines'. On an inside page the paper told how Lieutenant Burney, while still in his twenties developed the paravane, an invention which killed the menace of the enemy's lurking moored mines.

The paravane was a cigar-shaped cylinder with a vertical wing fitted to it to act as a rudder. It was towed by serrated wires outwards from a ship's side and kept at a depth below the surface unaffected by the vessel's speed, deflecting away from the ship any mines in her path and cutting their mooring wires so that they surfaced and could then be blown up by gunfire.

His paravane is reputed to have saved £100 millions worth of Allied shipping.

When the nation acknowledged its debt to inventors for their part in the victory, he was fortunate. In the distribution of awards most received less than £50,000 and were taxed. William Mills, who invented the Mills bomb, asked for a penny for each bomb, and since an estimated 76 millions of these had been tossed around, at 240 old pennies to the pound he would have been entitled to over £300,000; he was allotted instead £27,750. Sir Dennis was not included in the list; he sought no reward since he had been allowed by the Navy to patent the paravane, the commercial rights of which are said to have brought him over £250,000.

The naval lieutenant who often recalled he saved his first £100 with difficulty was thus rendered comparatively wealthy and enabled to pursue other objectives. One of these was to give Britain its first airship.

On his father's death in 1929 he left the Navy, ranked as a commander on the retired list. With the aim of persuading the Government to start an imperial airship service, he stood for Parliament and was elected MP for Uxbridge. He wanted to use the Zeppelins surrendered as reparations by the Germans, but upon asking Dr Barnes Wallis, one of Vickers Aircraft back-room boffins, to survey these, the hulls were found to be too corroded.

The Labour government which took office in 1924, however, decided to enter the airship field, and in an ensuing controversy over whether the State or private enterprise should build, one order was given to the State's aircraft establishment at Cardington and another to Vickers. Sir Dennis went into partnership with Vickers to build airship R100.

Dr Barnes Wallis, later famous as the designer of the World War II Wellington bomber and creator of the bouncing bomb with which the RAF Dambusters destroyed the Ruhr dams, became its chief engineer.

The stress engineer was a young man named Nevil S. Norway. When Norway was writing so assiduously in his spare time, Sir Dennis assumed he was compiling a mathematical textbook and was surprised when this turned out to be a first novel by Nevil Shute.

Despite that the private enterprise team started work later than the other, they were the first to complete. Sir Dennis crossed the Atlantic with R100 in both directions, and from time to time during the flight, at 3000 feet above the sea, he and Dr Barnes Wallis crawled in the full force of the wind along the narrow catwalk above the gasbags to observe the stresses.

He was in disfavour with the Government and was not included among the guests when the R101 airship which the State had designed and built left on a prestige flight to India. At 2am on 5 October, 1930, she plunged in flames into a forest near Beauvais, some 60 miles north of Paris, taking to their deaths all but eight of the 53 on board. The shock of the disaster halted all airship development in Britain; although the fault to which the crash was attributed was not present in the design of R100, the privately built airship was nonetheless scrapped.

A few years later Sir Dennis made sensational headlines in the United States when he took to that home of the automobile his 'streamlined car', to which he gave the same name as his airship. The R100 car was designed to reduce wind resistance to a minimum, and was the first car with an engine at the rear. The Prince of Wales bought one, but few others did, for it was large, powerful and expensive and it was left to the Germans to mass produce a small car based on its precept, which came to be known as the Volkswagen 'Beetle'.

At the start of the war against Hitler the War Office installed him at Ardeer with the staff of his little company he called Broadway Trust, and it seconded military personnel to help him. When he asked the Ministry of Production for someone with design and production experience to supervise the project, he chose from among the candidates William Lochridge.

William (Bill) Lochridge was 30, a creative and adventurous Clydeside engineer and draughtsman who had survived the years of the Depression in the engine rooms of old tramps, and was production engineer of five aircraft parts factories. Other attributes apart, what pleased Sir Dennis most was that the candidate he chose knew nothing whatever about guns, and thus would have no preconceptions.

The 8 inch gun, nicknamed the Drainpipe, was intended for the Army, but it was thought it could be used also in destroyers. Since the blast from its jets would have blown away the vessel's entire bridge, Sir Dennis designed a shield, rather like a snowplough, to be fitted on deck abaft the gun's jets, and to prove the efficacy of this he erected a dummy bridge on proving grounds beyond the fairways of Glasgow Golf Club's seaside course at Gailes.

The blast from the 8 inch gun did not blow away the dummy bridge, but the gun blew up during an official test at the proving ground. As Government and military observers scurried behind baffle walls, Bill Lochridge threw himself to the ground, taking with him an unwary official photographer. A ten-ton chunk of breech block fell a few yards from them, spattering them with earth and, he said, "creating a bunker as big as the members of the golf club might ever be likely to see."

The shoulder gun was meant to go to war in the Far East, but the atom bomb rendered its journey there unnecessary.

Long before then, however, Sir Dennis had begun what he told his staff would be "something for us to do in peacetime."

The 'something for us to do' might have taken Bill Lochridge with the inventor to Africa, for Sir Dennis had ambitions there. But Sir Dennis' immediate concern was rather with deep sea fishing.

Bill Lochridge had as few preconceptions about fishing as he had about guns, but then, Sir Dennis also had few, other than that he considered the fishing industry as less efficient than it ought to have been, which was why, after the nature of his plan was revealed to the staff, he and Bill Lochridge spent long hours in the Royal Scottish Museum in Edinburgh studying models of fishing vessels and nets and other gear and poring over books and papers far into the evenings.

Sir Dennis planned to send vessels to fish further away, and stay at sea longer than any British trawler had done, to fillet, pack and freeze their hauls of fish as soon as they were caught, and return to ports such as Glasgow, Liverpool and Manchester to sell in big stores and shops.

Not only had no one attempted an enterprise on such scale; the history of experiments to freeze directly at sea was calculated to stay the most adventurous.

Distant water fishermen of the time put to sea with a load of crushed ice in the hold to preserve their catches. By the 1890s a steam trawler with her ice load could reach Icelandic waters, and not long after could go beyond the Arctic Circle to the seas around Bear Island, and into the Barents Sea and its landlocked inlet the White Sea. But however larger and more powerful the distant water vessels had become since then, how far they sailed, and how long they fished, was circumscribed by the knowledge that fish kept in ice deteriorates in 16 to 18 days.

Mother ships fed by catchers were used before the war to try to defeat the distance barrier. In the 1920s Hellyer Brothers of Hull fitted brine immersion plant in two cargo ships which had plied the frozen meat trade, renamed them *Arctic Queen* and *Arctic Prince*, and sent them in summer season to Greenland to act with dory line catchers and to bring back halibut. In winter the vessels lay in port as floating cold stores, releasing day by day their stock of fish.

William A. Bennett of Associated Fisheries followed in the early 1930s, converting the 10,000 ton *Thorland* to send her to Greenland. She had a collier to fuel her, and liners and steam trawlers, some of which caught for her and others hastened home with the cargoes she had frozen. The cold store which Bennett built in Grimsby to receive their loads was the first sub zero store in the town.

J. Carl Ross, who later built up the Ross Foods empire, also entered the scene, financing a Danish expedition in 1935.

The financial rewards from these endeavours had been dubious. Moreover, transfers of catches had proved hazardous even in the comparatively good weather of summer. Since Sir Dennis intended to fish all year round, he quickly determined that mother ships would have no place in his plans. *His* vessels would fish and freeze for themselves.

"Really," said Bill Lochridge, "if we had known in the beginning as much as we came to know later I don't believe Sir Dennis would have attempted what he did. It all just grew like the house that Jack built."

Nevertheless, bold as his plans were, when Sir Dennis outlined them to Lord Woolton, wartime Minister of Food, and to Sir James Lithgow, the Clyde shipbuilder, both gave him their backing, and at a meeting in 1946 in Lord Woolton's top-floor office in Lewis' Stores in Argyle Street, Glasgow, they agreed to join with him to form Fresh Frozen Foods Ltd, registering it as a research company to qualify for tax advantages. Bill Lochridge, who accompanied Sir Dennis at the meeting, was appointed there and then to manage it, while continuing as manager of Broadway Trust.

From the outset two formidable problems presented themselves.

One was that, although having himself no more than a basic knowledge of refrigeration techniques, Sir Dennis had founded his project on the premise he could freeze directly at sea more successfully than anyone had done before.

The other was that since a vessel which would fillet and pack and freeze had to carry a factory crew as well as one to sail her, she would not be able to fish in the orthodox way.

Sidetrawlers (familiarly known as 'sidewinders') with their midships cut low to the water, turned broadside to wind and sea while their crews heaved catches up and over the bulwarks, in relays to obviate the risk of losing any of the catch. Sir Dennis' vessel would have a freeboard too high to do that.

Trawling from the stern was not entirely novel, but no-one had attempted it in the oft-mountainous seas of the North Atlantic, for that meant hauling in the net with one heave.

"Nonetheless," said Bill Lochridge, "if we were to fish at all we knew that's what we would have to do."

The search for solutions to both problems went on at the same time. Doubtless in the case of the freezer the quest would have led sooner rather than later to Torry Research Station, which the Department of Scientific and Industrial Research had set up in 1928 at Aberdeen as a permanent laboratory to investigate preservation of fish, but since work was continuing on the weapons development, the first contact happened when Bill Lochridge called at a little engineering workshop in the port, where a part was being made for the shoulder gun. The shop being close to the harbour, he engaged fishermen and merchants in conversation about freezing at sea.

They were unanimously scornful. But there were, they said, scientific folk at Torry who thought otherwise.

At the research station Dr George Reay, its director (or superintendent, as the title was then) received his visitor warmly as a newfound partisan of his cause.

Dr Reay and his predecessor, Dr Adrian Lumley, had advocated freezing fish at sea for a long time; and had sought to persuade British trawler owners, with, he had to concede, disappointing response.

Dr Reay had been at Torry since it began and had taken part in the first British experiment, when the Aberdeen trawler *Ben Meidie* was chartered and carried a small freezer during the summer of 1928 in voyages to the waters of Iceland and southwest Ireland. But after a report of the tests was circulated to trawler owners, Sir John Marsden, head of Consolidated Fisheries, which had one of the largest fleets, wrote to say he hoped freezing of fish at sea would never succeed; it would, he said, open up the British market to the world, people would get used to frozen fish and that would be a disaster for the industry.

Nor had anything come of a proposal by Torry five years later that the Government and trawler owners share in the charter of a trawler to freeze at sea for a year in a commercial experiment.

During this time there was one brave individual British endeavour. An owner sent out a trawler with a refrigeration plant and while it is not recorded how far she went it is known that she returned with her catch frozen solid, so that it was dug out with pickaxes. French, Germans, Norwegians and Danes tried too; one vessel, the German *Volkswohl*, specially built as a freezer with State help, operated her plant for a full year. But since she was then laid up as 'commercially unviable', the British trawling industry was not impressed.

Freezing techniques, however, had advanced far since early failures—"quick-freezing" had come of age.

10

The theory of quick-freezing had been propounded 30 years before. Fish frozen on shore—as it commonly was then in a low temperature chamber for 12 hours or more—lost appearance and taste when thawed because large inter-cellular crystals formed and changed the texture. But scientists found that if the fish could be passed quickly through the critical phase in which most of the crystals formed the harm could be minimised.

Dr Reay and his staff had defined criteria for quick-freezing as zero degrees to minus 5 degrees centigrade within two hours and storage at minus 20 to minus 30 degrees centigrade (temperatures not available in cold stores when first promulgated).

Although only a few processing firms in this country in 1946 had adopted quick-freezing, Dr Reay was sanguine. He had just brought in from Glasgow's Royal Technical College a young man named Gordon Eddie to inaugurate an engineering department. Gordon Eddie's first task was to design a freezer capable of being installed in a sidetrawler. With this Dr Reay hoped to persuade the trawler owners to accept the previously rejected year-long freezing at sea experiment.

His visitor left with fewer illusions concerning the difficulties to be faced, but with the promise of Torry help.

Among the several quick-freezing processes which had been developed, the greatest advance had been made by Clarence Birdseye, an American biologist and fur trader. On a hunting expedition in Labrador in the early years of World War I he tasted caribou which had been left a long time in the open, and fish as tender and fresh as when it had been caught by the Eskimos, and he realised that when it froze quickly in the intense cold the decaying processes were arrested while the cellular structure remained intact and both flavour and nutritional values were retained.

After eight years of experiment he perfected what became known as the multiple platefreezer. In this, trays loaded with fish could be placed in freezing cabinets between pairs of metal plates. When cabinets were filled a hydraulic press forced the plates and trays together and froze the fish into blocks. General Foods bought his company in 1929 for 28 million dollars (of which his share was a million). The invention fathered the frozen food business in the

United States. By 1946 it had already grown there to a large scale, though scarcely known here.

Unfortunately for Sir Dennis, Clarence Birdseye's platefreezer was designed for use on shore. It operated on direct expansion refrigeration gases and it would not be suitable in a heavily rolling ship.

Fred Schofield, Sir Dennis' chief draughtsman (later chief designer) continued their research. The design which then evolved proved a compromise between Clarence Birdseye's process and that of blast freezing, another method in general use.

The prototype plant, built for Sir Dennis at the works of L. Sterne and Co in Glasgow, was an insulated chamber, six feet high and four feet square. It was divided by shelves, each made up of a single layer of parallel tubes. Through these brine circulated, cooled by fans forcing cold air continuously between them. In first tests potatoes were used, these having a moisture content like that of fish, but later Torry provided fish from their research vessel, and Dr Reay was able to suggest several design changes.

Sir Dennis meantime found the trawling gear of his time wanting. The conclusion could have been reached *a priori*, for he had always intended to develop his paravane for more purposes than to foil the nation's enemies.

How it came to take its place in the concept was described by Bill Lochridge a few years later when he gave a paper to a conference of engineers and shipbuilders:–

The ordinary trawl, he explained to his audience, is roughly similar to a large string bag, its front end open to receive the fish, its rear end tapering to what is known as 'the cod end' where the fish finally find themselves.

The lower front edge of the mouth which slides over the sea bottom is known as the footrope; the net is towed by two wires, one from each 'wing' of this footrope.

The upper front edge of the mouth, called the headline, has numerous floats attached to it, and their buoyancy keeps the mouth open vertically.

Two heavy rectangular boards, called otter boards, are connected between the wings of the net and the towing wires or trawl warps in such a way as to present inclined surfaces to the water. Moving these inclined boards through the water results in an outward thrust which keeps the net open laterally.

"But," he went on, "a flat board is not the most efficient form of lifting surface, otherwise aeroplanes would employ flat wings. . . ."

The otter boards which thus found disfavour with Sir Dennis were discarded and he replaced them with a version of his paravane— using curved surfaces of aerofoil section—which he called 'parotters'.

With these he calculated the mouth of the net could be made to gape ever wider and swallow up more prey.

But he had another, longer term, objective. The heavily-armoured keels of the otter boards as they dragged along the bottom kept the net stable, but they did not allow trawling for other than demersal fish such as cod and haddock which feed at the bottom.

His parotters would not confine the net to the seabed as the otter boards did. They were to be the key element in what he hoped to develop as the world's first midwater trawl, catching not only the demersals but herrings and other pelagics which shoal at various depths.

Models of his parotters were built at the workshop in Ardeer and tried in an experiment tank at Denny's shipyard in Dumbarton, and tested by towing from motorboats in Ardrossan harbour.

The vessel then acquired to find out if they could trawl from the stern with the parotters at sea was a 200 ton steam yacht named *Oriana*. Built half a century before for the chairman of the old Glasgow Allan line of steamships, she had an owner's cabin and six guest rooms, crew accommodation and a saloon abaft the wheel-house.

Bill Lochridge located her laid up in the Holy Loch in the Firth of Clyde. He bought her for £1,200 and sailed her to Irvine harbour, acknowledging the wave of a uniformed man on the quay, to find on landing that this had been the harbourmaster trying frantically to convey that the bar at the entrance to the River Irvine was about $9^1/_2$ feet. *Oriana* touched bottom as she scraped over.

After her stern had been modified to a form of slipway and

chutes had been fitted to her side to accommodate the parotters, she began to trawl for fish experimentally in the Firth of Clyde.

The first parotter consisted of two cigar-shaped bodies, held together side by side like Siamese twins, but this was replaced by a single body made of sheet steel, in form like a dolphin, about 17 feet long and about 10$\frac{1}{2}$ feet high. It had a vertical wing which was about 60 square feet in area, shaped like an aeroplane's wing, and it had a stabilising tail.

The parotters were held on wires which shackled to the spreader wires of the towline, but they were towed separately, at a point fixed at the centre of pressure exerted on them by the water. Just as a child's kite will lift when the string is attached at the centre of wind pressure on it, so the effect was to pull the mouth of the net outwards.

Their streamlined buoyant bodies kept the parotters at about 20 feet above the net, only touching bottom if they encountered a sudden rise of contour.

But they still stayed stable.

Had the prototype freezer been ready before *Oriana*'s conversion was completed, it would have been installed in the yacht. Instead, an insulated box was fitted on her foredeck to hold her catches. Since she was not allowed to fish for profit, their canny manager bartered the fish for other gear.

The tests were adjudged successful. But the Firth of Clyde is not comparable with the North Atlantic, even if it can be rough betimes. *Oriana* was sold, and the search went on for a successor to fish in deep waters. She was found at Portland naval base.

HMS *Felicity* was a Canadian-built 1500 ton Algerine class twin screw minesweeper. When she was bought for £5000, Sir Dennis' son Cecil, who had gone back to Cambridge to read engineering, accompanied Bill Lochridge on a conducted tour of the vessel; at the end of this the young former junior naval officer derived wry satisfaction in informing *Felicity*'s three-ringer skipper: "Well, we're buying your ship." The £5000 gave them everything except her armament and the wardroom piano, and Bill Lochridge managed to sell one of her boilers to a brewery for £3000 and her refrigerating machinery to the manufacturers of it so that they received her at almost no cost.

Felicity was sailed to Sir James Lithgow's yard at Ardrossan to be converted, and she was named *Fairfree*. It had been intended to call her *Fairfreeze*—the first part of the name after Sir James' main yard of Fairfield in Glasgow—but the Registrar of Ships objected that the name sounded plural.

From just abaft her funnel, where a trawling winch was sited, the dockyard gave her a deck over her existing quarter deck. It was free of obstruction like an aircraft carrier's, but it ended in a stern built like a chute (and with a hump in the chute to prevent anyone going overboard). An afterbridge over the chute controlled her fishing operations. Trap doors on the deck opened to send her catch down to a factory deck below, which was equipped with fishwashing machines, filleting and packing tables, cod liver oil boilers and storage tanks, and a freezer twelve times bigger than the prototype.

While she was being converted, Sir Dennis flew to Africa to pursue a project which had been delayed by the war. This had been in his mind for 27 years; on a visit to Northern and Southern Rhodesia in 1920 he had stood at the awesome Kariba Gorge, where the Zambezi River narrows between hard rocks 250 miles below Victoria Falls, and had envisaged how the untapped wealth of the hinterland might be exploited if the river were to be dammed and its power harnessed.

Just before the conversion of *Fairfree* was completed he came back to Britain, and he told reporters the governments of Northern and Southern Rhodesia had agreed a plan to build together a dam and a hydro electric plant, and a railway to link the inlands to the coast. He had been given a concession to prospect for iron ore and coal over an area five times larger than that of Wales, he added, and two British steel companies were joining with him in a consortium to build a smelting plant. In the heart of 'the dark continent' there would be created "a new Sheffield".

Sir Dennis had also become the owner of a 20,000 acre estate called 'Little England' near Southern Rhodesia's capital, Salisbury. He told his staff that at Little England he would grow three crops of tobacco while his neighbours grew one, this by the expedient of damming a river as it flowed through his estate, and installing overhead irrigation.

In October, 1947, his floating laboratory was ready for public inspection at Ardrossan dockyard.

Before *Fairfree* undertook her maiden voyage he invited a large party on board. Government officials and scientists and engineers travelled overnight from London, and reporters came from daily and weekly newspapers and from trade journals. But few trawler owners were there, and the only company whose principals were encouraged by what they saw was the French firm of Marocaine de Pêcheries which operated off the coast of West Africa. It decided to convert its 150 foot long trawler *Mahbrouk* to take Burney freezing equipment.

To advance beyond *Fairfree* Sir Dennis needed someone with money and experience in ship operation.

The help was to come from a source he did not expect. . . .

CHAPTER TWO

When the war was over and there were pieces to be put together again there were few of them left for Captain Harold Keith Salvesen, head of the family partnership of Christian Salvesen and Co. and of its whaling and merchant shipping enterprise which traded as The South Georgia Co Ltd at numbers 29 to 37 Bernard Street in the old port of Leith.

The whaling fleet was in ruins. All the factory ships had been sunk as they carried planes and tanks and landing craft for the Forces. Half of the 53 catchers that had gone to the Navy, and the only modern tanker, had fallen prey to the enemy. Of the three survivors among the vessels which previously supplied the expeditions in the Antarctic, the only one usable was the 40 year old transport tanker *Saluta*.

Throughout the war Captain Harold had operated the vessels for the Ministry of War Transport with the help of brother Norman and a skeletal staff composed of James Beaton, who had been confidential clerk to the previous generation and had been with the company for as long as memory served, men beyond call-up age, and boys, and a Miss Christine L. Boyd; she was the first female in that traditionally male preserve, but was skilled in shorthand, typed letters better than any apprentice, and moreover could read Captain Harold's handwriting, with which qualifications she was to stay as his confidential secretary for another 24 years.

When the war ended Norman wanted to give up an active role in the partnership, and elder brother Noel, who had been Military Control Officer for the Scottish ports, decided to retire.

Harold's sole remaining partner was cousin Iver, who would come back from the Army to operate their merchant fleet. He, too, would have few pieces to pick up—all their nine tramps were gone, and only two veterans, aged 21 and 25, remained to restore their little Norwegian line.

Harold, who was 48, might have had a different life.

The company had been started as a shipping agency in Leith by grandfather Christian, who, one of a family of nine in Mandal in Norway, came to Scotland to seek his fortune and became a naturalised British subject. When Christian brought in his three sons, Tom, Fred and Theodore, as partners, Theodore (the youngest of them and Captain Harold's father) took the family into whaling, firstly in the Arctic and then in the Antarctic, establishing a land station on the island of South Georgia in 1909 and naming it Leith Harbour after their home town.

Harold had been introduced to whaling at the age of 12, when his father took him on a visit to the Shetland whaling station at Olna. The visit did not inspire him to follow in his father's footsteps. In 1914 he went directly from The Edinburgh Academy to Sandhurst, where he was prize cadet, and from there into the Indian Army. In campaigns in Mesopotamia and North West Persia he was twice mentioned in despatches. On leaving the Army, he took first class honours in economics at Oxford and then tutored there, but at the end of four years he yielded to his father's entreaties to come home to help in the family business.

The reluctant volunteer was referred to by all his staff as 'H.K.', or as 'Captain Harold'. He retained the military moustache, and the purposeful stride of the soldier, though he had begun to stoop a little.

He was no academic don lost to practicalities. The first whaling company owner to go down to the Antarctic, he was reputed to know every pipe and conveyor in the crowded machinery complex of his factory ships, in which he would prowl and probe for hours, accompanied by a chief engineer under his persistent cross-examination.

In the memories of those who knew him well he had many contradictions, for he could be forceful and challenging yet pleasantly persuasive, and incredibly generous while seeking to conceal it. He could also be critical and exacting, at times inducing apprehension, but he was sentimentally attached to those who served him

18

and was more indulgent to his 2000 British and Norwegian whalers than to any others; he knew most of them, and their family histories, their virtues and their weaknesses and foibles.

His warm rapport with them is known to have been tested just once. A group of flensers, exasperated by his persistent questioning, surrounded him with flensing knives raised over their shoulders. When they brought the knives down within inches of his feet he did not flinch. Honour was satisfied, both for them and for him.

His indulgence did not extend to bureaucrats in government. They were as pleased to see the back of him as he was to see the backs of them, for he did not suffer fools gladly and did not conceal that he considered them as in that category. Nonetheless he had cajoled the Government in the year before the war ended to give him priority to build two replacement factory ships.

Over a long time he had warned, as had his father, that greed would lead to the extinction of the great mammal. But little had been agreed to conserve its stocks.

When 13 nations met in Washington in 1946 to sign a convention regulating whaling the outcome fell far short of his expectations. The three major Antarctic whaling nations, Britain, Norway and Holland, adherents of pre-war agreements, signed as expected. But two others whom he deeply distrusted also signed; the war-defeated Japanese, who had spurned all regulation and were responsible for wholesale destruction of young whales, came to the table as supposedly repentant sinners, and the Russians were enabled to enter the Antarctic for the first time.

Although in the respite war had given the whale from its hunters stocks were recognised to have multiplied greatly, and although devastated Europe was hungry for the fats the whale could yield, the International Whaling Commission which was then set up, and which was charged with deciding an overall catch limit on scientific advice, authorised an excessive total.

The Commission also was given no power to enforce rules on the Convention members, and it set no national quotas, as Captain Harold had advocated. Instead, members were required on honour to report their catches accurately, the Commission calling halt when the overall limit was reached. In the free for all (with all the opportunities to cheat, as the Russians were subsequently suspected of doing) he saw inevitable further depopulation of the whales, and, among the industry's participants, the survival of only the most ruthless.

His scruples prompted him to propose price control to the Government and to his whaling rivals, and he bluntly told his shareholders, who were not many and like himself mostly descendants of the founder, that though they were spending on a scale "unprecedented in the company's history and uncommon in the history of merchant adventurers working as a private association," they should not expect quick recovery of their money. "You would not wish," he said, "that our products be sold at scarcity prices when in consequence of the ravages of war many people face starvation owing to the dearth of fats and proteins."

On VJ Night, 8 August, 1945, when rockets to celebrate the surrender of Japan flared into the night sky above floodlit Edinburgh Castle, the old transport tanker *Saluta* sailed out of Leith docks bound for the whaling land station of Leith Harbour in South Georgia.

Saluta had fuelled the convoy escorts and troop liners which had sailed in convoy from the Clyde. From among her crew and others there had been rounded up 180 men, vanguard of the several hundreds to follow.

Most had been down to the ice before, comrades of a band of 22 Britons and Norwegians left alone and for so long on the bleak island 800 miles east of the Falklands. The 22 had all volunteered to stay at the end of the 1940/41 expedition when the Ministry of War Transport decided the war against the U-boats was more important than whaling and it had requisitioned the factory ships and catchers.

Throughout the years of waiting and wondering when the war would end, they subsisted on supplies from their nearest neighbours, the neutral Argentinians at Grytviken base, several hours boatride away, and they spent the days shovelling snow off the roofs of buildings and tank tops to prevent cave-ins, manning a 4 inch gun and drilling with rifles as a unit of the Falklands defence force, under the command of Tommy 'Red' Laurenson, and listening at the radio station for warnings of the armed raiders which prowled the seas around, always menacing but never coming to test them.

Two new whalecatchers, *Southern Strife* and *Southern Truce*, had preceded *Saluta*. The weary old tanker transport broke down four times on the way, so that it was the end of September before the exiles' main relief arrived.

The youngest on board *Saluta* was 18 years old deckhand William (Willie) Greenfield, who had been an office junior at Bernard Street until Captain Harold offered him the opportunity to go whaling whenever war ended, and had sent him in preparation for this to the Leith training ship *Dolphin* and thereafter as deckboy on the fleet oiler *Coronda*, based in the Clyde.

Today he remembers seeing, for the first time, through flurries of snow, the glistening tops of Mount Paget and Sugarloaf and the triple peak of The Three Brothers (named after Christian's sons, Tom, Fred and Theodore), and a rampart of rocky cliffs that seemed to him impenetrable until out of it came the catcher *Southern Strife* to fuss her way around the transport before leading her into the bay; two toots on the station galley's steam whistle were then answered by a deafening blast from *Saluta*'s siren, and a motorboat came chugging alongside with some of the exiles, 'Red' Laurenson's brother Willie at the helm, this welcoming party to be greeted with the ribaldry with which old comrades often hide emotion—cries from the crowded decks of *Saluta*—"Where the hell have you been then? Didn't you know there was a war on?"

Surprisingly, most of the volunteers chose to stay with the expedition throughout that first postwar season.

Southern Venturer, first of the factory ships to complete, then arrived, bringing hundreds more who knew nothing of Captain Harold's fears for their livelihood, and even if they had known would not have believed them; for them, the war was over and the future was now. . . .

As replacements for brothers Noel and Norman, Captain Harold brought in the Hon R. C. (Ross) Geddes, heir to Lord Geddes, and T. H. (Tom) Humphreys, who had collaborated with him at the Ministry of War Transport. They were the first 'outsiders' to join the board.

He also recruited two members of 'family' (and soon after took them into partnership). Both had served throughout the war and had just been demobilised.

One was Noel's son-in-law, Clifford Marshall. He had been one of the first entrants when the RAF Volunteer Reserve was formed, had earned a DFC in action and had survived the tow of his flying boat from 100 miles out in the Atlantic after a forced landing.

The other has a principal role in *Fairtry*'s story.

Leonard Maxwell Harper Gow, known as Max Harper Gow and after his knighthood as Sir Maxwell Harper Gow, was a Salvesen on the distaff side; his grandfather was Theodore's elder brother Edward, who as Lord Salvesen was a judge of Scotland's supreme court, the Court of Session.

When war began he had completed his second year at Cambridge University. He joined the Ayrshire Yeomanry as a trooper but early in 1940 he was sent to the 125th OCTU (Royal Artillery) for officer training. Whilst there, the Germans invaded Norway. He volunteered to join one of the Independent companies as interpreter and served throughout the campaign to oust the invader, later taking part in the Lofoten Islands raid. Service followed with the Commandos in Europe and in North Africa, and with Lord Lovat's brigade in the Normandy landings.

Family tradition did not extend to pampering its eligible and chosen young. Although the Commando major had acquired a wife and he had a child to support, Captain Harold gave him a salary of £660 a year, a week's grace to take the honeymoon of which he had been robbed in wartime, and sent him to join the 1946/47 whaling expedition which was about to sail with the second factory ship, *Southern Harvester*.

In that whaling season the rival British factory ship *Balaena*, owned by Hector Whaling, carried among its expedition a team of scientists sent by the Government to find out if whalemeat could be added to the nation's diet.

The British public had voted Labour into power at the end of the war on a programme of reconstruction and social change, accepting to bear as the cost of its fulfilment another instalment of the stringent austerity that had been borne in wartime; food rationing continued, meagre but fair, the entitlement of meat paltry.

Balaena brought back an experimental 50 tons of frozen whale-meat in 1947. That year was a particularly bitter one. Power cuts, rationed coal, dark freezing nights added their miseries to the gloom. When the scientists enthused that whalemeat if fried with onions was 'indistinguishable from beef', the Ministry of Food happily gave its blessing to the importation of frozen whalemeat in bulk and began to extol its palatability and its nutritional values.

Thus encouraged, Captain Harold decided that he, too, would bring in frozen whalemeat cargoes, and he gave charge of this operation to Ross Geddes.

Ross Geddes' first thought was to use a corvette-type catcher, converting her for the purpose, but when he contacted Sir Dennis' Fresh Frozen Foods company for advice, Bill Lochridge declared this plan to be 'totally inadequate'. No refrigerating vessel that was large enough was readily available, however, except *Empire Raven*, a ship built by the Americans in World War I to bring home their dead. When Bill Lochridge was asked to inspect her refrigerating plant, the forthright engineer opined that it could qualify as a Kensington Museum piece. A contract was then given to Sir Dennis' company to equip the vessel with Burney freezers and cutting and sorting tables and spiral chutes so that she could process whalemeat in 150lb blocks.

While *Empire Raven* was being converted at Liverpool, where she was renamed *Southern Raven*, Bill Lochridge continued to sail *Fairfree* in the North Sea and as far as the Faroes, freezing an experimental 15 tons of fish per day, and hand filleting and packing it in 7lb catering blocks which he sold to hospitals and prisons and to anyone who would listen to him.

As he visited Bernard Street between voyages he was invariably invited to take Captain Harold's customary afternoon tea in the boardroom, and Captain Harold became more interested in Sir Dennis' fishing venture, encouraging his guest to talk much more of this than of what he was doing equipping *Southern Raven*.

That vessel's conversion had been completed when Captain Harold told Bill Lochridge he would like to meet his principal. It was some weeks before that could be arranged, but Sir Dennis returned from Africa and one afternoon in September 1948 he arrived at Bernard Street with Bill Lochridge and his *Fairfree* skipper Jim White.

If his ideas were too radical for the trawler owners, the techniques were not unfamiliar to Salvesen. They winched huge whales over the stern ramps of their factory ships, and compared with the complex processes on board these ships, it seemed simple to process fish liver and oil. Salvesen were also well acquainted with capital risk. Each expedition to the Antarctic took 300 to 500 men, each had to be stored and fuelled with as much as 40,000 to 50,000 tons of oil, yet despite all the precise calculations and forward planning that this entailed, fog or storm could ruin a season and luck in finding whales mattered as much as good judgment.

For over five hours Sir Dennis and his manager discussed with Captain Harold, Ross Geddes, Iver and Tom Humphreys if Salvesen could share in the project.

Sir Dennis wanted to negotiate a partnership, but Captain Harold did not wish association with anyone. In the evening he invited Sir Dennis to stay overnight at his home, where the two men continued their talks alone. Next morning they again talked alone, at Bernard Street. By then they had obviously reached an under-standing, because when the full meeting resumed in the afternoon Captain Harold at once asked everyone except Sir Dennis to leave the boardroom. Five minutes later the inventor emerged to tell the surprised Bill Lochridge and Jim White that he was selling Fresh Frozen Foods Ltd lock stock and barrel, with patent rights, and Salvesen wanted all the staff to join them.

"Nobody in fishing was interested," said Bill Lochridge. "He knew very well that some thought his ideas were crazy and that there were those who wanted them to fail. He couldn't take the concept any further on his own and he accepted that only someone like Captain Harold would be able to see it through."

Sir Dennis left immediately for Africa. Captain Harold gave responsibility for *Fairfree* to Ross Geddes and he flew to Rio de Janeiro to join a catcher which was on her way to Antarctica. He took with him his nephew Gerald (later Sir Gerald) Elliot, who was joining the company and would act on the tour as his personal assistant.

For the 25 year old recruit, whose career till then had closely patterned that of his uncle's—the Indian Army at the age of 18, captain's rank in the Frontier Force Rifles and graduation in economics at Oxford—the summons to go to the Antarctic initiated a two-year course charted for him by Captain Harold; following the tour of the expeditions he would train in whaling administration at Tønsberg, the whaling fleet's Norwegian base, and in shipping on secondment to a company in Liverpool.

Although the results of the first two whaling seasons were satisfactory, Captain Harold dampened whatever optimism they raised among his shareholders. Whaling, he warned them, faced 'a precarious future'.

In 1948 food allowances in Britain fell to their nadir—two eggs and two ounces of cheese per week, three or four ounces of butter and sixpennyworth of meat. But however impoverished was the nation's diet, however inured people were to substitutes, the cargo of frozen whalemeat which *Southern Raven* brought back from Antarctica found no welcome. The Ministry of Food proliferated recipes, but paradoxically it insisted that whalemeat could be sold only by fishmongers and that it should be labelled 'Whale' if used in sausages and pies.

Disposal of a second cargo was no more successful. Ross Geddes hawked it around as pet food as far as to the United States, and to Greece, while *Southern Raven* lay in the Holy Loch with a crew going nowhere until she was relegated to be used as a transport and finally sold for scrap.

CHAPTER THREE

Fairfree was sent to a Clyde shipyard and converted to diesel power.

Before resuming her voyages, she tested the parotters in the Firth of Clyde over a period of two days, towing them at different depths and at different speeds. Then in August 1949 the trawler which had been GW 19 and had become LH 271 made her first voyage beyond the limit of ice-provisioned trawlers—2500 miles from Port Glasgow to the Grand Banks of Newfoundland and 2500 miles back.

The Grand Banks is a submarine plateau, an extension of the Continental Shelf, stretching over 400 miles from east to west and 350 miles from north to south. Here where the Labrador current from the Arctic meets the Gulf Stream flowing up from the Caribbean, cod proliferate, and as much as 30 tons of haddock was known also to be taken in a single drag. Though too distant for the conventional British trawler, French and Spanish fishermen had come in the seasons of good weather for centuries, salting their catches. Portuguese schooners came too, with dories loaded on their decks, one atop the other like ice cream cones. These were lifted out at daybreak, and a man put in the thwarts with lines and a pot of bait, to be picked up again at nightfall.

There were no radar reflectors fitted to the dories then (as they were later) for the mother ship to locate them in poor visibility, so that sometimes they did not pick one up, the poor wretch being lost in a sudden squall.

The log book of *Fairfree*'s maiden voyage to the far grounds recorded mishap after mishap.

The filleting machine had not been designed specifically to work at sea. In its cycle of operation it first beheaded the fish, then carried it on its side on a rotating table past revolving knives. Self-centering guides held up the fish in accurate position for the cutters, which then ripped the fish on either side of the backbone, and at the sides of the triangular breastbone, until a fork arrangement pulled the fillet clear of the backbone.

In tests conducted while the vessel was berthed at Port Glasgow it had posed no problems. But in these tests the fish had been dead for 24 hours, rigor mortis had passed, the flesh was relaxed and the bone supple so that the fish was pliant when distorted by the curving movement of the table. The flesh of newly-caught fish being firmer, when the cod was fed into the machine at sea a ragged fillet ensued, or when the machine should have separated the flesh from the bone, the bone broke.

In the harbour tests also the vessel had been stable; at sea the self-centering guides failed to cope with her movements. Filleting on the voyage thus had to be done manually, and on return to port the machine was put ashore.

Though the engines were now diesel, the steam auxiliaries were retained. These had given no trouble during the vessel's comparatively short trips to the North Sea and the Faroes, but after ten days in the Atlantic water came over with the steam and put them out of action.

While trying to effect repairs, they made for St John's. As *Fairfree* came into harbour, and the engine room responded to Skipper Jim White's ring to go astern, the engineers could not at first see (the flywheels being screened by their guard covers) that the engines were still going slowly ahead, and *Fairfree* was finally stopped just a few feet away from the point at which she would have run down a Portuguese schooner and the terrified crew members on deck.

Soon after returning to the grounds, the same boiler troubles beset them; both the main and auxiliary generators failed, and to compound their misfortunes several small fires had to be subdued, including one in the galley that left them with no cooked food.

Fairfree set off back across the Atlantic with no electric power, handsteering in the steering flat and navigating with only a lifeboat compass (the magnetic variations of which they were unsure). A day off land, they hailed two fishing boats to explain their predicament, and the fishermen told them "Head as you are and you'll see Tory

Island."

Fortunately they met two destroyers as they made landfall, and these guided them into the Firth of Clyde—at which point the main generator came to life and they managed to reach Princes Dock in Glasgow unaided. There, its repentance complete, the generator once more gave up the ghost.

There was, however, a welcome discovery on the voyage. Most of *Fairfree*'s catches were being taken from the bottom, but the parotters' arrangement of towing wires did not permit—as did conventional otter boards—the use of a trailing ground wire, the vibrations of which help to shepherd fish towards a net. When they trawled from the stern with otter boards it was found that contrary to Sir Dennis' belief this could be done.

There was also ample proof of the limitations of the ordinary distant water trawler; one which kept company with *Fairfree* for a time had a quarter of her catch condemned on return to port.

Fairfree's first cargo from beyond the 'ice barrier' was sent in insulated vans 300 miles to Grimsby. More good quality fish such as was *Fairfree*'s was landed at Grimsby than elsewhere; the port was also the centre of quick-freezing in Britain, and Smethurst and Co, at whose factory the catch was thawed and then marketed, had most expertise in freezing techniques in the town. Salvesen knew the company well; it helped to supply the whaling expeditions. There was also a longstanding friendship with Smethurst's parent, the Unilever concern, which was a major buyer of whale oil.

Two ladies, habitually garbed in blue overalls, white mop cap, thick white woollen stockings and clogs, ran the Smethurst factory and its 1200 workforce. They were the Misses Margaret Swallow, its managing director, and Louise Gibb, a graduate analytical chemist who had been her deputy for 22 years. They were to prove good friends of the venture when later it encountered opposition, and from some even hostility.

Catches from each of *Fairfree*'s twelve more voyages went to Smethurst. But with each voyage losses mounted. The vessel was too small and cramped on her factory deck, so that fishing had to be halted periodically while the catch was dealt with, and her draught was too shallow to allow her to operate in severe cross

28

winds. She was plagued also with mechanical difficulties. On one occasion she set off bound for the White Sea and was forced to run into the Norwegian port of Trondheim with water pouring everywhere among the auxiliaries. After that it was decided that the Faroes was as far as it could be risked to go.

In June 1950 Ross Geddes resigned to buy two tankers with which to form Trident Tankers. Clifford Marshall and Max Harper Gow shared the departed director's duties, the former taking over *Fairfree*. These two were joined soon after by Gerald Elliot as he completed his two-year training course.

Hitherto Captain Harold had not confided to his two junior partners the depth of his forebodings over whaling's future, but he now deemed it time to tell them that it would not long endure, and new activities would have to be found to replace it. Max Harper Gow, having believed he was embarked on a lifetime career in that specialised business, was initially dismayed, for the only other 'new activity' was the *Fairfree* venture.

From the outset Captain Harold had accepted that that vessel was no more than a guinea pig; a larger, more sophisticated ship was needed if the project was to be viable. In July he took to the board a proposal to build one, and the board accepted his view— despite the protests of his brother Noel—that "the economic possibilities of fishing with refrigerating vessels justifies further risks."

In October he went back to the board, this time to seek agreement to build two ships. It was important, he told his fellow directors, to develop other lines. He regarded the quick-freezing business as "one with a big future, holding out the prospects of financial success for efficient participants." Noel dissented, but after a second meeting the board agreed with Captain Harold's proposal to build two ships rather than one. However, Captain White returned from a voyage to the White Sea and said he no longer advocated fishing there during the months of severe Atlantic storms, as had been planned. His fears were subsequently to prove much less well-founded than he supposed, for the new ship was so much more seaworthy than *Fairfree*, but since estimates had been based on fishing all the year round, Captain Harold reluctantly accepted that

29

only one ship be built after all.

Fairfree was laid up at Leith, near the Sailors' Home, in September, 1951, no one having been found willing to buy her. But in the three summers they had sailed her, their research had told them all they needed to know to design the new vessel. She was planned to be of 2600 tons gross, 281 feet in length overall and 44 of beam, to have a speed of 13 knots and to endure 80 days at sea— ten to the grounds, ten to return and 60 days to fish.

Captain Harold himself chose her name. She would be *Fairtry*. The name seemed fitting for a daring experiment.

Clifford Marshall, Bill Lochridge, and Percy Scorer, the company's chief superintendent engineer, set out to visit shipyards. They had a list of five; but the one they chose was the first that they visited. The yard was that of John Lewis and Sons, of Torry, Aberdeen, a family firm which had begun in the last century by building little river ferries and cobbles for a clientele which included Balmoral Castle, and had progressed till it could boast of having sent down its slipways into the River Dee more than 200 steam and motor trawlers, coasters and cargo ships. In 1951 the company was also operating a fleet of 30 trawlers.

The irony of their choice was not perceived by Salvesen, and possibly not also by Andrew Lewis, chairman of the shipyard company and grandson of its founder, but it did not escape the notice of the yard's near-neighbour, Torry Research Station. When Torry had first asked the trawler owners to join in the test to freeze with a chartered vessel from the fleet, the late Sir Andrew Lewis (father of Andrew) had been one of the few who had even troubled to reply. Sir Andrew said he doubted if the plan could succeed, and he went on: "If times were better we might take a chance, but as things are we dare not . . . it is really a case of being first to venture, and as you know, the pioneer invariably loses money."

Clifford Marshall, who alternated with Max Harper Gow as the director accompanying the whaling expeditions, left for South Georgia in the early autumn of 1950/51. When in his absence several changes were made in the ship's plans he objected so strongly to these that on his return he said he wished to be relieved of responsibility for the project. (And after an unrelated disagreement with Captain Harold he resigned a year later).

Max Harper Gow, who then inherited charge of *Fairtry*, at once faced a dilemma. Estimates had been based on freezing the bulk of her catch as whole fish, but however long he studied these he could not reconcile them with the operating costs; it seemed to him that the only way to make the vessel pay would be if he could concentrate on filleting and use the offal as fishmeal.

There was considerable doubt if this could be done—the bid to fillet mechanically at sea on board the predecessor *Fairfree* had failed.

Rudolph Baader, the inventor of the filleting machine, still believed, however, that he could design one that would work successfully on board *Fairtry*.

Baader was the 'father' of mechanical fish processing. He was an engineering visionary who 12 years before had set up a research institute in a little workshop in Lubeck, Germany's chief Baltic port, and three years later introduced to the fishing industry its first herring filleting machine. He had sent two of his senior mechanics with *Fairfree* on her troublesome maiden voyage to the Grand Banks; their observations had spurred him to develop further, and in place of Fairfree's model Ba 88 he designed a new unit which he called the '99'. Unlike the earlier machine, which carried the fish radially, this conveyed the fish to the cutters in a straight line.

Bill Lochridge had seen it work in Germany—on shore. But no one would know if Rudolph Baader's confidence was justified or was misplaced until the machine went to sea, and whoever took it would do so as an act of faith.

It was delivered to the Smethurst factory in the winter of 1951 and when Max Harper Gow saw it in operation he decided to accept that Rudolph Baader was right. He would install it in *Fairtry*.

He and the inventor became good friends during several visits afterwards to the Nordischer Maschinenbau factory at Lubeck. During one visit, Baader adapted the model so that it could deal with haddock and whiting. For this success he was indebted to *Fairtry*'s chief engineer Jim Campbell and 2nd Engineer Johnny Adams, who, together with Bill Lochridge, were there to train in the repair and maintenance of the unit to be installed in *Fairtry*.

31

While on the training course the two engineers decided to experiment on their own. They marked out a cam outline from the bottom of a butter tin, and with a skeleton of a large haddock in the gripper, they handcranked the machine and proved the outline correct. Baader then made a solid cam and found that it worked.

Another concern arising from the decision to concentrate on filleting remained, however.

Six freezers of Sir Dennis Burney's design were to be installed. These froze whole fish well, but when they were tested on fillets, using the Burney prototype plant at the Glasgow factory of L. Sterne and Co (the firm installing *Fairtry*'s refrigerating plant) the freezer could not give them a flat block of fillets which would fit into a carton.

Clarence Birdseye's platefreezer could have provided an answer. But that had been rejected as impracticable at sea.

Max Harper Gow decided to find out if it could be adapted. When he visited Birds Eye's headquarters in London with his problem, the engineers there who were presented with the challenge designed a version which circulated cold brine through the plates, and the invention with which Clarence Birdseye had inspired a land-based industry was enabled after all to go to sea.

Fairtry would carry three Birds Eye units to deal with fillets, while three Burneys would freeze whole fish.

Lewis' shipyard laid the keel of the new vessel in August 1952. Until construction would be more advanced, little remained that required Max Harper Gow's attention before he was due to join the Antarctic expeditions again.

As he left his Grimsby base at Smethurst's factory, the British fishermen were engaged in a confrontation with their Icelandic counterparts which was to go on sporadically for a quarter of a century and was to have a disastrous ending for the distant water fleet.

The little northern republic, which lost nearly a quarter of its fishing fleet by enemy action as it helped to feed us in wartime, had nonetheless profited sufficiently from the war to rebuild its fleet, and it extended its three mile limit to four. More than that—whereas Britain had always based claims over her seas as extending to three miles from low water mark line to the nearest point on the coast, and considered the sea beyond that to be free, Iceland drew point to point lines across the bays of its 3730 miles of coast, shutting off some of the richest fishing in the world.

Some in the industry were prepared to concede the need to conserve stocks. But where, others asked, could it end?—Peru and Chile were claiming a ludicrous 200 miles limit!

The trawler owners, who controlled all landing facilities at the ports, effectively banned all landings of Icelandic fish. Iceland retaliated by refusing shelter and repair to British vessels.

Grimsby was a tense and tetchy port to which Max Harper Gow would be bringing searching examination of long held tenets. . . .

33

CHAPTER FOUR

The Grimsby to which Max Harper Gow returned in 1953 differed greatly from the town as it is today.

One of Grimsby's landmarks is a 300 feet high rectangular tower nearly a century and a half old, which could be taken as a replica of the Torre del Mangia, the noble campanile of the Palazzo Pubblico in the heart of Siena. But although Grimsby's tower is in the style of that historic Gothic structure, it overlooks no sunny piazza; it stands at the sea entrance to the docks, starkly exposed to the rude North Sea winds, and its original mundane purpose was to house the hydraulic machinery which operated the dock gates and quay-side cranes, and to hold 3000 gallons of fresh water to pump supplies to the ships and to dockside houses.

In those days, had you climbed its tortuous stairs to the lantern top, you could have seen hundreds of vessels below. It is said that at times one could almost cross a dock on their decks.

Grimsby was base for more than 90 distant water vessels, more than 100 middle water vessels, and for seine netters and inshore boats besides.

As many as 8000 people worked in the streets around, where smoking sheds and drying sheds, with flues and slotted shutters, warehouses and factories, little and big, huddled cheek by jowl in intimate rivalry. In the mile-long covered market, known locally as the Pontoon, 400 merchants jostled and shouted. Ten to fifteen trains with long wagon tails left the railway sidings and through the night unhitched loads consigned to 600 stations all over the country.

Here was a veritable town of its own.

Since the general adoption of quick-freezing after the war there had grown up also in and around the town a frozen food business—in Grimsby rather than in Hull on the opposite bank because

34

beyond Grimsby lay the fertile hinterland of East Anglia, so that into the town came peas and other vegetables and fruit to add to the fish that was being processed in the refrigerating plants.

Grimsby also had Tickler's jam factory, and Dixon's big paper mill, a biscuit factory and timber import yards. But it depended for its livelihood mainly on fish, as it had done since the far-visioned directors of the old Manchester, Sheffield and Lincolnshire Railway developed the fish dock exclusively for fishermen and invited smackowners of the southeast coast to come and land their catches and send them to London free of dues.

The fish trains have gone. Beeching's axe on the railways accounts for that rather than the decline of fishing; the last train left the port on 1st January, 1967, and Grimsby relied thereafter on insulated lorries, complemented later by refrigerating vehicles. Grimsby has penetrated further into the plain, and there is an industrial spread along both banks of the river.

If you tried to walk across a dock now on the decks of the boats you would not get far without falling into the water. But Grimsby in the 1950s could claim to be the metropolis of the fishing world. Hull might dispute the premier title—its distant water fleet out-numbered that of Grimsby—but Hull was based on the cod which its fleet brought in, while into Grimsby came also a harvest of plaice and haddock and halibut.

Most of the trawling companies were family concerns with a dominant figure at the head.

The most powerful was William Alfred Bennett, chairman of Associated Fisheries Ltd, a group of companies which employed more than 3000 people in trawling, processing and distribution. He was known to everyone as Big Bill.

Big Bill was 6 feet 4 inches tall, built in proportion and with an outsized personality to match. A man of much warmth and good humour, but withal forthright and accustomed to his own way, he was held in affection by most and in awe by others.

He had built up his business from modest beginnings. As a 14 year old, he wheeled barrows from 5am in Billingsgate market for his father's firm. Ten years later, while with his Army unit in France in the last years of the 1914–18 war, he was told of his father's death. The Royal Artillery officer came home to take over the business with its staff of eleven. He had £300 capital and a loan of £1000 from his father's estate, and an avowed aim "to make the name of Bennett known", which he proceeded to do with remarkable rapidity.

His trawler fleet which sailed from Grimsby, Hull, and Fleetwood in the 1950s outnumbered that of any other concern in the world. While he controlled the group from headquarters in London, his vessels in Grimsby were operated by his son John and those in Hull by Tom Boyd, son of his old friend Tom Boyd senior, owner of the Boyd Line. John Bennett and Tom Boyd were almost as brothers; upon demobilisation—John from the Army and Tom from the Navy—John lived for several years with the Boyds as one of the family in lodgings in bombed-out Hull while old Tom nurtured their entry into trawler management. At the end of their tutelage John went to Grimsby to take control of his father's Northern Line while young Tom ran Bennett's Lord Line in Hull.

Big Bill Bennett had never sailed in any of his ships. "There never was a bunk to fit me," he would say.

His closest rival—and the most influential figure in Grimsby itself—was J. Carl Ross.

Carl Ross, like Bennett, had begun with modest resources. When he was 18 years old, his brief career as a naval wireless operator was ended by the Armistice of 1918. He signed on a freighter in Hamburg intending to see the world, only to find his ambition thwarted by a phone call from his merchant father to come home and fill the boots of a much older brother who had quit the business. For ten years after that he bought and sold fish on the Pontoon until his ailing father handed over the firm to him.

He had no formal training in accountancy, but his comprehension and judgment in matters financial soon became legendary, and by the age of 52 he had transformed the business into a huge enterprise. He also had a fleet of more than 50 middle and distant water vessels, some of which he secured by acquisition from several of the trawler barons and others he had had built to his own order.

Neither Bill Bennett nor Carl Ross was personally antagonistic towards Max Harper Gow. In wartime transit camps a friendship had been forged between fellow Commandos Max Harper Gow and John Bennett, and Max Harper Gow had also known Tom Boyd from meetings at Dartmouth, where the young naval officer commanded MTBs co-operating at times with the Commandos in raids. But both Bill Bennett and Carl Ross, though they would figure directly later in *Fairtry*'s fortunes, stayed aloof in business.

Of the other owners, the most notable were Sir Fred Parkes and his son Basil, who operated the Boston Deep Sea Fisheries fleet out of Hull and Fleetwood, the Hellyer brothers Graham and Mark, the Marr brothers Geoffrey and Leslie, the Hudsons, and the Watson Halls who ran the Thomas Hamlings and Co Ltd line.

The impending invasion of their industry by the vessel building in Aberdeen was disturbing, but it was of less immediate concern to them than the dispute which had introduced such growing rancour between themselves and the Icelanders. This was exacerbated in May by the intervention of self-made millionaire George Dawson, who flew to Iceland and signed a contract to take the Icelanders' fish at a fixed price for five years.

He planned to land his first cargoes at Grimsby in October. The owners were as determined that their boycott should hold and his cargoes go elsewhere or back whence they came. Jack Vincent— locally dubbed 'Fighting Jack'—who shared managing directors' duties with his chairman Carl Ross—was taking a leading part in securing a solid front against Dawson.

The stranger from Leith, installed with his papers and plans in Smethurst's old wooden boardroom, could not expect any of the owners to wish his concept well.

To take a factory to sea to fillet and pack and freeze was a long march into the future. It bypassed a major part of the industry's operations. In addition, to trawl from the stern turned around completely shipbuilding design, this at a time when with the help of Government grants and loans no fewer than 47 sidewinders had been built with years of usefulness ahead of them, and 22 more had been planned.

For many of the owners even to freeze at sea was itself a step too far.

In 1953 they could not be held to be as blinkered as Sir John

Marsden had been. All of them acknowledged the basic weakness of the industry's economy, that dependence on crushed ice meant a skipper could spend perhaps only half his time actually fishing before having to return with a hold only part-filled, while the risk-taker tempted to stay too long on the grounds paid even harsher penalty. They could scarcely fail to recognise the weakness in the face of the disquieting totals of condemned fish landed from time to time.

But they saw costs of freezing at sea as burdensome, techniques imperfect, and an established cold storage chain ashore lacking, and they had looked rather to more powerful engines to reduce the time spent not fishing, and to the development of better trawls.

Nevertheless Dr Reay had worn down resistance. He had secured permission—albeit with misgivings on the part of some owners—to conduct a survey at sea in which for two years his spartan Torry scientists shared the hardships of the deepsea fishermen; Gordon Eddie in the time had designed a first vertical platefreezer which had been tested in hundreds of day trips in the North Sea; and finally Dr Reay had presented this before the industry as able to be installed in a sidewinder.

With the influential backing of the White Fish Authority (which the Government had set up shortly before "to regulate, reorganise and develop the industry") the owners were persuaded in 1953 to accept the plan to carry out a year-long freezing at sea experiment.

A sidewinder chartered from the distant water fleet and converted to take a production model of Gordon Eddie's freezer was to sail 'under normal trading conditions', managed by her owner but under the technical and scientific control of Torry staff, landing her early catch after each voyage to be stowed, thawed and distributed from a cold store ashore.

Addressed as this plan was to answer the problems of an existing sidewinder fleet, it was, of course, far removed from the *Fairtry* concept.

Fairtry was launched by Mrs Harper Gow on 30 June, 1953, watched by large crowds. She was the biggest and heaviest vessel to have been built on the Dee, and the yard had to take special precautions against mishap.

38

On the Humber her arrival was awaited with uneasiness on the part of many. An inventor three years before dabbling in a tough industry could be dismissed as an eccentric; in 1953 a wealthy concern was about to encroach on hitherto untouched preserves with a challenging new type of vessel which might well prove to be the forerunner of others.

After her launch Max Harper Gow began to recruit his crew. He needed not only experienced fishermen and seamen but engineers more skilled than those carried by other fishing vessels. He also needed, as a consequence of the decision to concentrate on filleting, 20 more factory hands than before. Filleting was traditionally done by women; he contemplated quartering them down one side of the ship and men on the other, but he abandoned the idea as too difficult.

The factory crew were found mainly in the Humber ports and in Aberdeen. Most had never been to sea, but by union agreement they could be called on to work on deck if needed, and if they became skilled could ask to change from factory to deck. Persuading experienced fishermen to join was more difficult. The British deep-sea fishermen would endure the rigours of Arctic's dark winter cold and heaving seas and drifting floes for as long as three weeks, but many were disinclined to exchange their three weeks of separation from the warmth of home and family to spend nearly two months more at sea, in whatever greater comfort than normally. Better pay and incentives had to be offered to overcome their reluctance.

The most serious lack for this exceptional vessel, certain as she was to pose so-far-unencountered problems, was an experienced fisherman to command her, one with patience and talent. Traditionally one did not entice fishing skippers to leave the companies which employed them, and Max Harper Gow spent sleepless nights wondering where he might find one. The attitude of most owners gave him little hope of an answer. Two among them, however, who were open to conviction that *Fairtry* could provide lessons from which they might profit were the twins Geoffrey and Leslie Marr. Max Harper Gow in desperation was about to seek a skipper from abroad when Leslie Marr came to him with an offer. It was motivated, said its recipient later, "by a nice mixture of generosity and enlightened self-interest."

Fairtry would be lent one of Marr's best skippers for a year so that the vessel could have a fair start. During the year the skipper would be free to give Marr the benefit of the expertise he acquired, and at the end of the year he could choose whether he would stay with *Fairtry* or revert to Marr's employ.

Leslie Marr then brought Leo Romyn to see Max Harper Gow, and the deal was sealed with a handshake all round.

Leopold Dixon Romyn was 52 years old. He was one of Hull's most successful skippers.

His upbringing had been more privileged than that of most with whom he shared the uncompromisingly hard life of the trawlerman. His father had retired from the teaching staff at Jesus College Cambridge at the age of 40 upon inheriting part of the family estate; his mother was the daughter of an admiral and the niece of another. The boy was taught at first by a governess, then sent to a preparatory school in Sussex and finally to Lancing College, where he took Highers in Latin, Greek and Ancient History.

In 1920 he embarked on a business career with a firm of shipbrokers in Hull but upon finding office work uncongenial he signed on as a 'decky learner' on a Hull trawler. While an intellectual background is of little account working on storm-swept decks, being over six feet tall and powerfully built as he was he not only endured but rose to his own command.

He was fearless. Sailing with Romyn, so one described it, "alternated between periods of great admiration and abject terror."

When war broke out he sailed as RNVR lieutenant in command of the minesweepers *Rowan* and later *Rolls Royce*, was credited with having swept 197 mines and had been awarded the Distinguished Service Cross and bar. Once, when on leave from his command, upon a mine being sighted in the surf off Bridlington beach, he donned rubber boots, waded out and pushed it ashore to where it could be safely despatched. When he was asked why he did it, he answered, "I had to. My house was on the top of the cliff."

Leo Romyn called his new employer 'Gaffer' and Max Harper Gow called him 'Skipper'. Their association was to last not just for one year but for more than twenty.

But if Max Harper Gow could sleep more easily, a formidable worry remained for him—there was entrenched prejudice to overcome in the market *Fairtry* would invade.

Many merchants did not think that fish should be frozen at all. Eight years of peace had not eradicated among them or their customers memories of the frozen fish which had constituted much of wartime diet.

Fish was one of the few protein foods exempted from rationing in wartime. The Ministry of Food bought all the supplies, allocating them at fixed prices to the merchants (and did so until 1950). It also set up distribution zones based on the ports of Hull, Grimsby, Aberdeen and Fleetwood, so that anyone living far from a port seldom saw fresh fish (and often the housewife's only reward from the family was 'Oh not cod AGAIN!').

The Navy requisitioned from among the fishing fleets the more modern and larger vessels. The waters around Bear Island and Norway were cut off, and minefields dictated where else the remaining vessels could operate. Worn and patched and of uncertain age as some of the remnants were, they continued to fish in defiance of U-boats and planes and surface raiders, at first without protection, later in companies with two of their number armed. Since 85 vessels were sunk by U-boat gunfire, air attacks and mines, the fact the catch was even a third of what it had been was testimony to their gallantry.

The bulk of our fish came instead from Iceland, and from the little islands of the Danish dependency Faroes, which our forces occupied. The more intrepid of the Icelandic fishermen landed at our ports, but a large proportion of the Icelandic supplies arrived in carriers chartered by the Ministry of Food. Inshore catchers landed their hauls to be loaded in the carriers and stored in ice till the vessels received their full loads, layer on layer often crammed into the holds without regard to the fish at the bottom.

The Ministry took all Iceland's exportable surplus of frozen and salted fish, and if the public disliked the salted cod, its most unpleasant recollections were of the slow-frozen fillets which when defrosted tasted like wet flannel.

The belief among housewives had thus become common that if

fish was frozen this was because it was of too poor quality to sell at quayside auction.

Four months before *Fairtry*'s building was due to complete, the last important recruit arrived in Grimsby. Edward (Ted) Sealey would sell her catches.

Ted Sealey began his career as a boy with Islington Co-operative and he had sold everything from vending machines to soap before he had joined the Government-sponsored Herring Industry Board. As area supervisor for the Board he had latterly covered the West Country organising 'Herring Weeks' and window-dressing displays in a bid to popularise frozen herring—an experience which had left him with no illusions as to the extent of the public's resistance to frozen fish.

His arrival coincided with an attempt by the White Fish Authority to persuade the merchants to accept a formal freezing scheme. But in the cycles of gluts and scarcities there was a preponderance of gluts and when the British Ports Wholesale Fish Merchants Association met to discuss the plan they announced they were 'totally opposed'. There was no surplus at major ports suitable for freezing, they said; fish to be frozen ought to be of good quality and if good quality fish was taken this would denude the trade of its best supplies.

In such a climate fewer doors opened to Ted Sealey than when he had promoted frozen herring. Many refused orders, and others who irrationally expected fish frozen directly at sea to be much cheaper than fish landed by the fleet as 'fresh', stipulated "Only if the price is right."

Fairtry, the pioneer

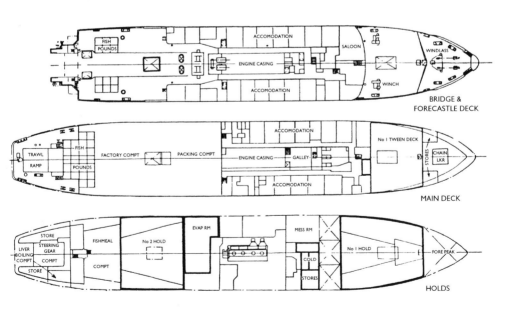

General arrangement of *Fairtry*

left:
Sir Dennis Burney

right:
Captain Harold Salvesen

Mastered Hun Submarines.

Lieut. Chas. D. Burney, R.N., only son of Admiral Sir Cecil Burney. His scheme for dealing with the submarine menace is, according to Admiral Sir Hedworth Meux, now being carried out at a cost of some millions. (Photograph exclusive to the *Daily Sketch*.)

above:
Seaplane trials
"at Lieut Burney's expense"
–Milford Haven, August 1911

right:
Front page news,
from Sir Dennis' scrapbook

The AUTO — MOTOR JOURNAL

The R.100

Broadside view of the "R.100" Burney car, showing the rearward mounting of the engine.

CAR of Individuality

THE very last word in motoring, as conceived by Sir Dennistoun Burney, the designer of the famous airship R.100. Its patterning actually is based on the streamline principles of that airship, in an endeavour to reduce wind resistance to a minimum. Consequently fuel consumption also is considerably reduced, while a greater proportion of the mechanical power than normally can be devoted to speed demands.

Below: The roomy luggage locker, accessible from top or sides. This between-ways compartment still further prevents engine noises reaching the car's occupants.

Above: Sir Dennistoun Burney, the designer, with his remarkable invention. It is equipped with an eight-cylinder engine, and gives accommodation for seven passengers.

Below: The engine, mounted over the rear axle, showing also the twin radiators and the efficient method of additional air cooling and expulsion of fumes.

Above: How the spare wheel is carried in the doors, and safely under lock and key. The car, it is claimed, is capable of exceeding the 80 m.p.h. mark easily.

Below: One of the new "Burney" cars on the road. Its size can be gathered from the baby Austin nearby. Several in fact will soon be seen on the roads.

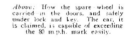

left: The shoulder gun on its transporter carriage

right: Sir Dennis' 7 inch recoilless gun

left: The big gun—despite mishaps, the War Office did not abandon development of it until 1948

above: *Oriana*, a dwarf compared
with what was needed

right: The stern arrangement
for *Oriana*—very different
from that of other yachts

left: The parotters

above: *Southern Venturer—Fairtry's* techniques were not dissimilar

left: Stern ramp operation, different dimension—in the Antarctic, huge whales were winched on board

above: Bill Lochridge (*right*) and his chief engineer Jim Campbell

The former minesweeper *Felicity* became trawler LH 271

above: *Fairfree*, converted to diesel power, on trials in the Firth of Clyde

right: The otter board—tests proved it was possible after all to use them while trawling from the stern

left: The launch of *Fairtry*

"Skipper"
Leopold Dixon Romyn

Sir Maxwell Harper Gow

below: At work on the deck of *Fairtry*—Leo Romyn is on the far right of the picture

On one of *Fairtry's* early voyages Bill Lochridge took this series of photographs to illustrate how the gear was handled

top: Cod ends at the foot of the slipway

left: At times when the load was too heavy, Leo Romyn would go down the ramp with a knife to cut the mesh and kick clear some of the fish

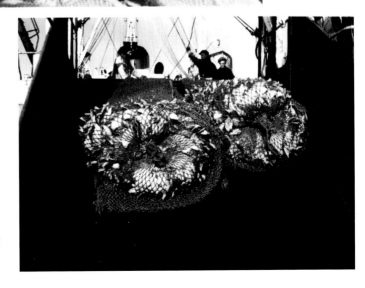

right: The cod ends being hauled on board

above: Cod ends on deck

left: Willie Greenfield
during a voyage on *Fairtry II*

above: In the late 1940s, a group of Smethurst long serving staff—Miss Swallow is fourth from the right in the front row. Joe Ward is first on the left in the front row, and Miss Gibb is immediately behind him, first in the back row.

above: J. Carl Ross, "the man with the midas touch" (*Picture: Grimsby Evening Telegraph*)

left:
William A. ("Big Bill") Bennett, colossus of the fishing industry

above: An old friend—*Fairtry II*, which became mother ship to mini submarines, first as *Vickers Voyager*, then when sold five years later to British Oceanic, as *British Voyager*.

left: On the deck of the *Lord Nelson* —John Bennet (*on the left*) with Tom Boyd and the late Sir Hugh Fraser (Lord Fraser of Allander)

above: The *Lord Nelson*—described as "a half-way house, a cautious probe into the future"

above: The launch of the *Lord Nelson*—the first
stern trawling freezer to have been built for
a British trawler owner

above: "Home from home" for half a century—Leith harbour base in the 1950s

Barry Sealey and his father Edward (Ted) Sealey

Sir Gerald Elliot—a world wide search...

CHAPTER FIVE

The vessel which was the subject of so much speculation among fishing experts throughout the world was completed in April, 1954.

Was she the vessel of the future?

The role of the factory ship was debated twice in the year before at congresses of the fisheries division of the United Nations' Food and Agriculture Organisation, in Miami and in Paris. Max Harper Gow and Bill Lochridge attended the session in Paris, and both took part in a discussion which followed presentation of a paper by David Cunningham, who had been general manager of John Lewis and Sons' yard during the early construction of *Fairtry*.

No valid comparisons with *Fairtry* were possible. Since 1922, when a wooden bulk freighter built during the Kaiser war had appeared as the *Santa Flavia* to can salmon off America's Pacific coast, this reputedly first factory ship had been followed by a procession of other conversions that ranged from cargo ships and ferries to tank landing craft.

Of contemporaries that could be cited, none except one had been specially built or fished for herself. The Norwegian *Clupea*, a former transport ferry, operated out of the Danish port of Esbjerg, fed by seine netters as the first herring meal and oil floating factory; the *Pacific Explorer* was a bulk carrier converted as mother to tuna and other catchers in the Bering Strait and Pacific; the *Africa Queen*, commissioned by the Colonial Development Corporation for tropical waters, operated with dory catchers off Africa.

The exception—the American vessel *Deep Sea*, half the size of *Fairtry*—was a modified trawler which normally trawled from the quarter off Alaska for king crab to can but also froze and filleted other fish. At best she was a distant relative if she could be called relative at all.

Fairtry was unique.

During the debates one expert, Morgen Yul, former chief fisheries technologist of the Food and Agriculture Organisation, observed that he had seen "more cases of failure in floating fish factories than in any other field of fisheries enterprise."

Most withheld judgment. One thing however was clear: as the noted marine engineer and naval architect A.C. Hardy pointed out a year later—"Whatever future development may hold, it seems to have gone too far to be dismissed as an ephemeral trend."

Fairtry ran her acceptance trials off Aberdeen during the Easter weekend. Her fishing tests, off Kinnaird Head, where there is a rare trough, ended abruptly when her trawl snarled on one of the many wartime wrecks. On a conventional trawler the snag would have been apparent at once, but such was Fairtry's power that nothing was noticed until the net was hauled on board, broken.

Guests at the trials were impressed by her. She had all the innovative features of the *Fairfree* conversion, but there the resemblance ended; she had the raking lines of a big motor yacht, a clipper stem and a cruiser spoon stern. Twice as big as *Fairfree*, she carried 600 tons of fuel to last three months at sea. As well as cod liver oil plant, she had the fish meal plant *Fairfree* had lacked, and could carry 600 tons of whole fish and fillets in her hold. She was powered by a Doxford diesel, carried the most modern navigational aids and other sophisticated equipment, and had as much electric power as to light up the *Queen Mary*.

The editor of *Fishing News* wrote:– "She is a wonderful ship and undoubtedly introduces the possibility of a new revolutionary era into deep-sea fishing."

When she sailed on her maiden voyage on 28 April some among the owners predicted quick demise for her, others that her impact on the scene might be less than prophesied.

The ports' struggle with Dawson was over by then. It had been brief and decisive. Seven ships landed 1400 tons of Dawson's fish at Grimsby in the space of five weeks, but Jack Vincent so effectively organised the boycott that only one man bought, and that imprudent merchant thereafter found that the trawler owners would not sell to him. The Cockney financier retreated; the factory he set up was deserted, its night watchman sacked, the phones cut off, and it was put up for sale, relic of a futile tilt against an industry which could close solid rank in the face of threat.

The dispute with Iceland, however, was going on regardless.

Fairtry sailed far westward of Iceland's waters, to the Newfoundland and Greenland grounds.

Max Harper Gow accompanied Leo Romyn and Bill Lochridge on the voyage.

To fishermen accustomed to sleeping and eating crowded together in a fo'c'stle *Fairtry* provided agreeable contrast.

On the bridge deck were the master's and radio operators' cabins, and a hospital room. On the upper deck, the deck officers, chief engineer and his officers and five others had single cabins and eight others shared two-berth rooms. On the main deck two people had cabins of their own, 14 shared two-berth cabins, and 48 fishworkers occupied four-berth rooms.

There were showers and wash places, hot and cold running water and a slop chest sold sweets and chocolate, cigarettes and razor blades—though almost everyone grew a beard.

However much Leo Romyn approved of his crew's comforts and was solicitous for their welfare, he scorned ease for himself. He stood always on the bridge, and said he would throw overboard any chair that was provided for him.

The crew quickly found that he was fair, but was a strict disciplinarian. To the dismay of some, he insisted on holding Sunday services. Bill Lochridge remembers that everyone sat on a life-jacket to cushion against collision with a neighbour on the pitching deck of the crew's mess room, while the skipper conducted a service in which Anglican, Presbyterian and Catholic adherents chose the hymns on alternate Sundays.

No liquor was carried, except for a few firkins of rum from which the skipper could dispense a ration at his discretion. Leo Romyn was himself a non-drinker—on a voyage some years later, when he discovered that a rum barrel had been broached, he ordered the barrels to be brought on deck, and he threw them one by one into the sea. As they bobbed away on the waves, a horrified crew watched in silence.

The mess deck could be used as a cinema. The first film was no box office blockbuster; it was a training film which Bill Lochridge had recorded while he was on *Fairfree*. There was also the usual shipboard library, of course, but most just wanted to sleep when off watch.

Mail arrived by courtesy of the little Newfoundland trawlers *Blue Spray* and *Blue Foam*, which hung a canister like a milk churn on a dan buoy that was fitted with a radar reflector. In the first delivery by *Blue Spray Fairtry* almost lost her manager overboard. After the crew made three abortive attempts to grapple the dan's trailing line, and Leo Romyn threatened to leave without the mail, Bill Lochridge leaned out from the bridge ladder with a boathook. The good fortune was that the hook went through the eye of the buoy. The bad luck was that the ship was going ahead, however slowly. He says he wonders to this day if those who grabbed him and secured a line to the boathook did so over concern for him or for the mail.

The parotters were tried briefly once more, and discarded in favour of the otter boards.

Hauls were gratifyingly heavy. Sometimes too heavy. Powerful as was the winch that dragged them up in single lifts over the stern, it strained alarmingly. Bags from time to time stuck on the ramp, and tore or burst, as critics of stern trawling had prophesied.

They pouched the fish into two cod ends to try to distribute the loads. (Sir Dennis had used four on *Fairfree*, and in those early days skippers who learned of his stratagem described it scornfully as 'towing a cow's udder').

The gear became caught too often—and damaged—as they encountered rough ground. Max Harper Gow described the tears and snags as 'seemingly endless'.

"We even had to go into St John's for other nets," he said. "Everyone had set out on the voyage with high hopes and enthusiasm. Then we hit those problems. I wasn't surprised to find teething troubles. You expect them in a new ship. But Leo was a bit downcast when he came home. Not that he intended to do other than carry on—he knew like the rest of us we'd beat the troubles. But he realised some things would have to be rethought."

Bill Lochridge said the strains on the winch were not a problem in themselves. "But the winch traverse gear," (which lays the wire evenly across the drum) "was too flimsy. We braced it ourselves and it held out till we got back and had it renewed. Then on later voyages we fitted a spring-loaded device to the winch so that it slacked off wire till the ship could be halted and the gear cleared of obstruction.

"So we eventually arrived at the most efficient methods by trial and error."

But as long as four years after this, Leo Romyn felt impelled to comment in a voyage report that no way having been then found to distribute the load by splitting the bag, any haul that was of more than twelve tons could often damage the gear "even if it does not tear it off clean at the becket and slither, cod ends fish and all, down the ramp into the sea and disappear forever. Nothing is more provoking than to see this happen or the cod ends burst and the sea be covered with dying fish.

"If one fails to gauge the towing time correctly and overdoes it, one is faced with the decision whether to try and get them all in or take a knife fastened to a long pole and let some out."

Three Baader mechanics were on board to tend their unit. The only problem it posed was that when it was washed down with salt water this caused corrosion; on later voyages this was remedied, the parts being replaced with stainless steel.

Rudolph Baader did not live to see his machine take its place among the technical advances of the sea, nor to know the spread of his name throughout the world's fishing industry. In the summer before *Fairtry* sailed, he died, at the age of 68, leaving his son Rudolph and his son-in-law Johan Diestel, to carry on his work.

While the filleting machine problem was past, however, another difficulty emerged.

Whereas the flesh of fish caught and kept in crushed ice in conventional trawlers was left white when the microscopic blood cells drained away, *Fairtry*'s frozen filleted fish retained the blood, and a brown tint developed.

This was to prove an unexpectedly sore travail when the filleted fish came to be presented to the trade.

No one competed with them throughout the time they were on the grounds, though the Spaniards reported having sighted for the first time two Russian trawlers, the *Odessa* and the *Sevastopol*. The crew of *Fairtry* little knew the two Russian vessels were an advance scouting party, probing the ground for big brothers still to come.

The voyage was otherwise uneventful, except that they had to make a detour in the final days to dodge icebergs.

By then Max Harper Gow had flown back from St John's to await her arrival in the Humber.

On 28 July she berthed at Immingham commercial docks—her draught was too deep to allow her to come directly to the fishdock at Grimsby—and she landed 290 tons of fillets in 7lb packs, 170 tons of whole fish, 86 tons of fishmeal and 4200 gallons of liver oil.

Ted Sealey had hired a queue of lorries half a mile long to take the cargo to cold storage in Grimsby. "No one had ever seen anything like it," he said. "I ended up myself on the backs of lorries handling cartons to keep the line moving."

Next day at Smethurst's he arranged a gathering of important distributors, and samples of *Fairtry* fillets were laid out for them to inspect. When the potential customers saw the unusual characteristics of the fillets many were appalled and it was a doubtful group which moved into a special room to sample the cooked fish.

Fairtry's fillets and other fish had been steamed and without garnishment or condiment were laid out on tables. When the *Fairtry* fillets were cooked the bloodcells disappeared, and, each sample being labelled with a code, only the kitchen staff knew which was which. Everyone chose the *Fairtry* fillets as best in flavour and texture.

But although some confirmed orders, most were convinced that the fillets would be unacceptable to the trade, and Ted Sealey had many more cancellations than orders. He sent out leaflets to explain the colour—"Those so-called fresh fish are not fresh fish at all," he protested—but as he trudged round caterers and shops the reception was even more discouraging than on his previous pilgrimage. Schools and hospitals and large-scale caterers would take frozen whole fish though few would do so at premium price. But in the shops most considered the fillets were suitable only to the frying trade which could conceal the colour, and uncomplimentary fishmongers told him from behind their marble ramparts "Take it to the fish and chip shops."

Smoked fish gave no encouragement either. Willie Carnie, the Granton owner, who had smoked some samples of *Fairfree*'s haddock for Max Harper Gow, declared them to be "Absolutely delightful. Never tasted better. But you'll never sell them." And so it proved, because while the fish from other vessels assumed a glaze when smoked, fish frozen at sea did not.

Everyone at Smethurst's believed in the ultimate success of the operation and—as Salvesen found later—they sold at a loss to develop the trade. In their laboratory Miss Gibb sought to bleach the fillets with lemon juice and other concoctions, to no avail.

On her second voyage *Fairtry*'s trawl picked up so many rocks brought down by melting Greenland glaciers that they had innumerable net breaks. Nevertheless they brought back 540 tons of fish—more than they had done on her maiden trip, and that in fewer days.

The voyage after that was made in one of the worst winter storms for many years. *Fairtry* was fortunate, suffering no more damage than having her bridge windows smashed in. On other grounds the British fleet lost 74 men in one horrific spell of four weeks.

On her fourth trip she brought back a new mate—Jim Cheater, a Newfoundlander who was married to an English girl.

Jim Cheater was to make a valuable contribution in this venture in which he found himself by chance. He was a replacement sent from Newfoundland to the ship when, ten days out from the Humber, the mate who had sailed with them collapsed during a boat drill and died before they could reach port with him. The mate had been signed on at the last moment and it was only when they landed his body at Burin, in Placentia Bay on the south east coast of Newfoundland, that it was realised no one knew his religion. He was buried in a Church of Scotland service on the basis that he had mentioned to a crewmate he had married in Govan Parish Church in Glasgow.

There were no rivals to be seen as they fished and the hauls were heavy. But the filleted fish they brought back sold little better than before. Max Harper Gow joked to his salesman he would "have to take the fish round in a barrow," and certainly these were days to dishearten even the enthusiastic Ted Sealey.

On the maiden voyage, however, when Max Harper Gow had landed at St John's he had found the port astir over a new form of processed fish which had been developed first in the United States.

These were fishsticks—or fish-fingers as we have come to know them—little oblongs of white fish covered in batter and breadcrumbs.

The industry in Britain received the news of them with scepticism. A headline in *Fishing News* reporting the phenomenon said 'Britain Not Worried About Fishsticks'. It continued: "The question is whether it will presage a similar development here. . . . English traders will see a similarity in essence to fish and chips . . . it is safe to say that were it felt they offered a new product suitable for this market they would soon be produced . . . the fishcakes already produced by some firms may possibly be the British answer to fishsticks."

The doubts were to prove unfounded. . . .

Fish-fingers were also to be the first of a chain of events that would influence the outcome of Captain Harold's *Fairtry* experiment.

50

CHAPTER SIX

Fish-fingers were launched in Britain by Margaret Swallow at Smethurst's under the Birds Eye label—with the *Fairtry* fillets so many in the industry had spurned.

They were the catalyst that made a giant out of the adolescent frozen foods industry which had been growing up in Grimsby. After them were to come other convenience foods, beefburgers and steaklets and pies and ready dinners of pizza and other ethnic foods.

Colonel William Smethurst is acknowledged as the earliest pioneer of the industry in Britain; in Grimsby lore it had its genesis at his factory with Miss Margaret Swallow's fishcakes.

The reader is already acquainted with Miss Swallow as the managing director of Smethurst's.

In the years of recession after World War I she was governess of 12 year old Honor, eldest daughter of Colonel William and Mrs Smethurst of Thornton Hall, when the family lost their trawler fleet and shipyard, and their only remaining asset, the small salt fish exporting factory in Grimsby's Ropery Street, seemed also doomed.

The young governess persuaded Colonel William that he could replace his lost trade with fishcakes made from recipes she used when she served the children with their afternoon tea; Honor was packed off to boarding school and the colonel took Miss Swallow into the factory.

Many fishmongers were making fishcakes at the time, but most of them made the cakes from fish left over from the previous day. If Miss Swallow's fishcakes were to have the wide distribution projected for them, their shelf life had to be prolonged. They were steamed in ham cookers at the factory to sterilise them, covered in batter and crumbed, put in trays and dipped in hot fat, and then passed through an air tunnel to cool.

51

They sold for 1$\frac{1}{2}$ old pence each; the colonel took the first samples in his chauffeur-driven car to seek orders in Grimsby and in towns around.

As early as 1926 the factory's talented chief engineer, J. B. (Joe) Ward designed a form of air blast freezing tunnel so that the fishcakes could be preserved to be sent as far as to Cornwall, and three years later the colonel installed a pilot freezing plant invented by White Russian M. T. Zarotschenzeff. When he asked the town's merchants to join in developing a commercial plant, no one would take the financial risk, so he acquired the European rights and built his own plant. Its installation in July 1931 is chronicled as inaugurating commercial quick-freezing in Britain.

In 1937 the little company froze poultry and in 1938 it was the first in Grimsby to freeze peas.

The colonel's trade was with caterers and institutions, hotels and restaurants and shipping companies. No one was developing frozen foods here as Birds Eye and others were doing in America. When in 1938 Robert Ducas, head of an engineering concern in Rochester, formed a company to manufacture Clarence Birdseye's platefreezer and to use the name under licence from General Foods, he chose an ill-time; on the outbreak of war the Ministry of Food banned development as 'inessential'.

Contrastingly, the Ministry exhorted Miss Swallow and her deputy Miss Louise Gibb to greater effort, and at the requisitioned factory in Ropery Street, in an office which the colonel converted for them as a bedroom, the two women lived throughout the war, on duty 24 hours a day, even taking their turns of rooftop firewatch, while they turned out millions of fishcakes to feed the Forces.

The ban on development did not deter Unilever from taking a controlling interest in Ducas' Birds Eye company. But they had to promise the Government to undertake no development of the business until the war ended. In 1946 they also took over Smethurst. Colonel Smethurst was dying; whether in the sale he made any stipulation concerning his loyal staff neither Miss Swallow nor Miss Gibb ever learned, but in any case Unilever wisely left the two women in charge.

Housewives were spending little more than £500,000 a year on frozen food at that time. Home freezers were almost unknown and such few cabinets as were in the shops were all of the enclosed 'coffin' type, mainly devoted to ice cream. So unhappy had been the public's experience of frozen fish that many thought the business would have no future comparable with that in America, if it had future at all.

In the years from then until the advent of fish-fingers the gloomy prognosis was disproved. The number of firms that quick-froze in volume, like Smethurst did, mushroomed.

Among the foremost in the development were the two biggest trawler owners, Bennett and Ross.

Bill Bennett had been freezing fish in the factory he built for Thorland's pre-war cargoes. He built another factory when the war ended, to freeze peas and other vegetables and fruit. Then in 1954 he absorbed a burgeoning business which traded under the brand name of Eskimo. With it he took into his group J. B. (Joe) Sprott and A. H. (Mick) Coburn, the two young men who had built up the business from humble beginnings in a converted railway refreshment room on the old herring slipway, and he translated them to a new factory at Royal Dock.

Carl Ross' entry into the business came when the Ministry of Food at the end of the war offered larger allocations of fish to merchants who would deep-freeze against scarcity. He was quick to seize the opportunity, hastening to America to see Jack Stone, inventor of a platefreezer rival to Clarence Birdseye's. He secured the British patent rights for £125,000 and began to manufacture it and to sell it to others.

The first machine was installed in 1947 at the little country parish of Westwick in Norfolk for a company formed with Alex (later Sir Alex) Alexander, a Czech refugee fruit farmer. A year later Ross built a large automated factory—unique of its kind in 1948—on Grimsby's South Quay to fillet and to freeze fish.

But while Bennett and Ross and others concentrated on the wholesale and export trade, Birds Eye, once freed of wartime restraint, turned, as it had long intended, to the retail trade, backed by the faith and resources and mass marketing expertise of parent Unilever. When it took frozen food into the shops in open top display cabinets so that housewives could see frozen food at a glance, the demand which resistant grocers had thought barely existed became very apparent indeed.

In the autumn of 1954 George Muddiman, the then chairman of Birds Eye, and his technical director, Ken Scamell, visited the factories of General Foods (which still had a minority holding in the British concern), and they returned with fishstick samples, sketches, drawings and specifications, and set up pilot lines to test the market.

Just a few years later, frozen fish would go into one end of an automated line and come out of the other as tens of thousands of fish-fingers every hour. As remembered by Robbie Blair, who was a senior executive with Smethurst (and then Unilever), Ken Scamell's first pilot fish-fingers were battered and crumbed, and popped into wire baskets in batches of about twenty to be dipped into a small frier.

But Birds Eye had no real frier of its own, and it fell to Smethurst as companion Unilever company to undertake full scale production on their behalf on a co-packing basis.

Margaret Swallow and Louise Gibb and Joe Ward could have found irony here; long before, they had filleted fish, removed the side (or pin) bones by hand, frozen them into slabs, cut these into triangles, breaded them and sent them to America. "Many people said that the idea of fishcakes and of the triangles merged in the concept of fish-fingers, and they could have been right," said Louise Gibb.

Ken Scammell chose to make his fish-fingers with *Fairtry* fish because in America there had been complaints initially that some fishsticks had been produced from fish of uncertain quality, and he was determined this would not happen in Britain.

They arrived in the shops in 1955 priced at 1s 8d (about eight new pence) for a ten-finger pack—"No bones, ready cooked," said the advertisements.

Their impact was dramatic. Rationing had ended barely a year before; the British public, wearied of restrictions and queues and ersatz food and lack of choice, had voted the Tories back into office, and for four years controls had been steadily diminished. Hairshirt days were over. To wives who were working in this time of full employment fish-fingers were a godsend—"Just take them out of the packet and pop them into the pan," the instructions said. Children, even those to whom fish had been anathema, loved the new boneless fish.

For Max Harper Gow they could eliminate one of his most worrying problems, since the discolouration of the *Fairtry* fillets, as we have seen, did not exist when cooked.

"But the Baader machine did not take out pin bones," said Max Harper Gow. "Freezing fillets at sea had only become practical because of the Baader machine. To be suddenly needed to produce fish-fingers seemed as big a leap as it had been from freezing whole fish to freezing fillets.

"It doesn't take much imagination to visualise a crew working on board a heaving ship—unlike skilled people in a spotless factory on dry land—trying to extract every little pin bone. The only practical way I could see was for us to macerate the fillets into mince, freeze them as a block of different dimension to what we were doing, and that could then be sawed up ashore.

"But that had then to be sold as boneless. The first child that had a bone stuck in his throat, or swallowed one, then we'd be in real trouble."

In any case, he had first to find out if a block of a size suitable for fish-fingers could be made on board *Fairtry*.

Smethurst were making the first fish-fingers with *Fairtry* fillets by defrosting them and taking out all the little side bones by hand. The fillets were then being macerated, packed in a large tin tray like a plasterer's float, a lid closed over and the fillets frozen again as a one-inch thick slab which could be guillotined into fingers.

Fairtry froze her fillets at sea in much deeper trays, divided into sections that had greaseproof paper in them. When these were filled the overlaps were folded over, the fillets frozen and tapped out as 7lb blocks about $2^1/_2$ inches thick. The blocks were then stored in cartons designed to fit into spaces in the hold.

Max Harper Gow asked Bill Lochridge if he could make a block suitable for fish-fingers.

At this time Bill Lochridge was about to leave to rejoin his former chief Sir Dennis Burney in a new fishing venture.

Sir Dennis had found much less ore in Africa than he had supposed. The two Rhodesian governments *were* going ahead with the building of the Kariba dam, a project that meant the creation of a huge lake, the re-settlement of 57,000 Tonga tribesmen, and—in an operation appropriately called 'Noah'—the evacuation of thousands of wild animals. But on finding there was no part for him in that great enterprise, he had come home to set up a research fishing company in collaboration with Sir Murray Stephen, chairman of the Clyde shipbuilding firm of Alexander Stephen and Sons Ltd, and with the trawler owning Hellyer brothers Mark and Graham.

Bill Lochridge agreed that before rejoining Sir Dennis he would make a last voyage with *Fairtry*.

He made stainless steel moulds of the correct size, packed these with pieces of fish, and left on board the vessel ten tons of evidence in blocks before begging a lift on a drifter to take him to Newfoundland and from there to fly home.

There remained the problem of the pin bones. Until the machines on board could remove them, Smethurst would have to thaw the fillets and take out the bones by hand.

Ted Sealey by this time had an office which consisted of three rooms and a kitchen (and a shared toilet) on Marshall's Wharf. He kept samples in the kitchen in an old chest freezer which had been used originally for ice cream. When he asked for furniture the office manager in Leith sent him two ex-Ministry of War tables. He had a typist, but the only other help came when his son Barry came home on holidays.

He went on one of *Fairtry*'s voyages because, he said, "It's a great company for experience," and he transferred from her to a little fishing boat which took him into Newfoundland. "And I must have looked a rare spectacle when I was dropped off *Fairtry*," he said. "There I was in the Atlantic getting into a small boat, dressed in the traditional travelling salesman's garb of black coat, and holding on to my Homburg hat."

For Ted Younge, Salvesen's technical director, what he remembered most when he sailed with *Fairtry* was an abiding sense of loneliness.

But there was soon to be no more loneliness for *Fairtry*.

CHAPTER SEVEN

In late 1955 there came into the North Atlantic a vessel which could have been taken as *Fairtry*'s sister ship.

She was Russian.

The crew of *Fairtry* could scarcely believe what they saw. Neither could the staff at Lewis' shipyard when they saw pictures of her.

Ted Younge did not share their astonishment, because a year after joining Salvesen he had visited Baader's factory at Lubeck and had gone on to Kiel, where the Howaldtswerke yard was building for the Russians. He had seen there the shape of what was to come.

The ships were known as the Pushkin class. "But *we* came to call them the Fairskis," he said.

They were the same dimensions as *Fairtry*, and their power was also the same. They carried 18 more crew however—including women, for the Russians had no reservations such as Max Harper Gow had had.

How did the Russians copy *Fairtry*?

Enquiries came from eleven countries after the minesweeper *Felicity* was converted as *Fairfree*. These included Russia. The concept of *Fairfree* then was set out by Bill Lochridge in general terms in a paper, published and readily available, which he read to the Institution of Engineers and Shipbuilders in Scotland in April, 1950.

When her successor *Fairtry* was ordered from Lewis' yard, Bill Lochridge planned her in outline on the drawing board at his home in Airdrie, and two people then translated this plan into final design.

One was Andrew Lewis, who had trained as a naval architect before entering his father's business, and had succeeded his father in 1950.

The other was David Cunningham, who had been a lecturer at

Glasgow's Royal Technical College and deputy manager at Fairfield shipyard on the Clyde before going to Aberdeen. *Fairtry's* construction had barely begun when he left to become general manager of the Brooke Marine yard at Lowestoft—and it was in that capacity that he gave his paper on factory ships to the Food and Agriculture Organisation fisheries congress in Paris.

The Russians doubtless gave particular attention to the paper, and to the contributions to the discussion by Max Harper Gow and Bill Lochridge, though both took care not to divulge detail of *Fairtry's* features.

Stalin died in March, 1953. He was not long in his tomb in Red Square alongside that of Lenin (though Kruschev later removed him to a lesser place of honour) before a chink appeared in the Iron Curtain.

Among the trade prospects that the Russians offered in the mini thaw was a programme of 20 trawlers and seven factory ships. The British Government pursued a policy of "expanding trade within the limits of security as an aid to peace."

John Lewis and Sons was asked to tender for the factory ships, and Brooke Marine of Lowestoft for the trawlers.

Russian interest in Brooke Marine seemed to lie in a type of trawler which Brooke Marine had built four years before for Icelanders. Called by her Icelandic owners *Jorundur*, she fulfilled the qualifications the Russians sought for fishing in Arctic waters.

The late Harry L. Dowsett, chairman of the engineering group which owned Brooke Marine, flew to Moscow in August, 1953, accompanied by his personal assistant Robert C. Battersby (later a Member of the European Parliament) who spoke Russian fluently, and by joint managing director E. R. Fry, and yard manager David Cunningham.

The delegation returned with good prospect of building at least one and possibly all the 20 trawlers the Russians wanted, but since the Admiralty thought that a vessel like *Jorundur* could be converted as a minesweeper, Harry Dowsett had to await Government clearance before proceeding further.

Clearance came in November and in the following month he took his delegation back to Russia.

Meantime, Andrew Lewis had a request from Moscow to send a set of plans for preliminary study, and he and Max Harper Gow were in a quandary. *Fairtry*'s stern arrangement was patented. But Max Harper Gow had not much faith the patent could hold, so he urged that the plans should not be handed over until there was a firm order, and if that failed, to ask for a sum for the plans, this to be shared by Salvesen and the shipbuilders as return for development costs.

The Russians replied that their regulations forbade payment until a contract was signed.

"We decided to blank out the stern in the general arrangement we sent," said Andrew Lewis, "and we told the Russians this was special gear but if they ordered the ships they would probably get it."

The two who went to Moscow to represent the yard were Gordon Milne, who had succeeded David Cunningham as general manager, and engineer-draughtsman Andrew Brodie.

Gordon Milne had begun his career as a 16 year old apprentice in his native Aberdeen, won a university scholarship at the age of 20, graduated with honours in engineering and naval architecture at Glasgow and was a Lloyd's surveyor before joining Lewis.

"I didn't go myself because the Foreign Office advised me not to," said Andrew Lewis. "The Government was concerned to foster trade but they didn't trust the Russians. I asked an old friend to go with Gordon Milne and Andrew Brodie to act as their general adviser and to liaise with the embassy."

The old friend was Percy Sheriffs, a wartime surgeon commander who sailed with a Shackleton expedition when he was a teenage Boy Scout, had never grown beyond 5 feet 4 inches and had been flyweight boxing champion of the Scottish Universities.

The three arrived in Moscow in freezing January as the Big Four powers conference on partitioned Germany was about to begin in Berlin. The Brooke Marine team had preceded them by several days, and were staying in the same hotel in Red Square facing the Kremlin, though as rival shipbuilders they did not fraternise.

Throughout the visit Gordon Milne felt uneasy, that he was being watched, and he was glad of Dr Sheriffs' presence as comrade and confidant.

A week went by before the first talks began at the offices of the Ministry of Foreign Trade. His unease was heightened by an incident while on the way to one session. Andrew Brodie found he had left his briefcase at the hotel and Dr Sheriffs said they had best return for it. The driver of their cab, who had given no hint of understanding English, at once turned the cab. At the hotel Dr Sheriffs told the other two: "we talk no more business anywhere except we go for a walk."

Of course, as Andrew Lewis said on reflection, Dr Sheriffs, the little man who sat alongside the other two from Aberdeen and took no part in the discussions, could have been suspected by the Russians to have been a British agent.

"We talked to them for four hours at a time," said Gordon Milne. "On each occasion they had a big team waiting for us round the table at the Ministry, as many as twelve, including a naval architect, a refrigeration expert and other fisheries people, all obvious experts in their fields; I formed a high opinion of their technical abilities. They had a woman interpreter there, but from time to time some of them spoke in English.

"The contract terms were most one-sided and our shipbuilding association had advised me I must get them modified. The Russians even inserted a clause stipulating that any dispute should be settled by a Moscow court. I wanted at least a neutral one and I offered the International Court at The Hague, but they would not have this.

"They kept asking technical questions while refusing to talk on contract terms. They must have had a fair idea of the ship from the general arrangement but there were things they were hazy about and they pursued these all the time.

"I did not give them any drawings. I was getting nowhere. All the talk was directed towards expanding on the technical detail of the drawings they had. So finally I said I would have to go back to the UK for further consultation. That was really an excuse to get away. They had taken my passport and had given me a temporary Russian one, and I did not get my own back until it was handed to me at Moscow airport. We never heard from them again."

The Brooke Marine delegation meantime were occupied

drawing (and re-drawing) for the Russians the plans of their own class of trawler, and preparing detailed quotations. But after the Lewis delegation left, the Russians told Harry Dowsett they wanted not only 20 sidewinders but ten factory trawlers of the *Fairtry* type, and they asked him if he could build six of the ten factory vessels in addition to the 20 sidewinders.

The precaution taken to blank out the stern ramp on the *Fairtry* drawings had been in vain, as Andrew Lewis had feared.

The Russians put a general arrangement on a desk in their office for the Brooke Marine group to study. Robert Battersby's recollection is that "It was not *Fairtry* but similar and larger, on heavy blue paper and in English."

The Russians told the group: "We can't hand it over to you," but, he says, "We studied it for about half an hour. What we saw had the whole thing there, the ramp and everything."

Brooke Marine's yard was really too small to build the factory ships. On the mudflat where they had built the *Jorundur* they had designed a wet dock and six slips with cranes that would create what Harry Dowsett said would be 'the most modern in Britain'. But even after they were completed, he would have had problems with the length of the factory vessels in one of the slips.

"However," said Robert Battersby, "we started to sketch our own. I can still remember with Harry Dowsett drawing my first ship on the floor of our hotel room. David Cunningham had worked on *Fairtry* and knew both her and the sidewinder, but we hadn't the drawings more than half an hour and we were just doing mock-ups.

"We were given a month to decide if we would quote for the stern trawlers. We felt we really had to start on conventionally known vessels, so we declined the stern trawlers and got the 20 sidewinders.

"The Russians could have pieced a lot of things together. Don't forget they were talking to us as well as Lewis and asking us to do it. Papers were probably looked at, rooms bugged. Anything you might leave in a room was examined and if any drawings were left they would have been photographed."

Harry Dowsett told the Russians he might try to form a consortium to build the factory vessels, and on return from Moscow he told reporters he was prepared "to make our plans available to other shipbuilders in Britain who might be interested, so that they can take up where we left off."

But the Russians did not place the order in Britain. It went instead to the Howaldtswerke yard at Kiel.

For the perspicacious Alexander Ishkov, the Soviet Minister of Fisheries, intent upon fast-feeding an undernourished nation, the Pushkin class that began in the German yard opened wide the door to the high seas of the world, and the ships that followed the Pushkin ultimately surpassed in number the fleets of all others.

How the Russians secured the plans is unknown to this day. Whatever the truth, they paid nothing for them.

Ten years after the John Lewis and the Brooke Marine teams were in Moscow, the last chance to unearth evidence fell to Bill Lochridge.

He had spent three years with Sir Dennis' research company and had then managed the biggest shipyard and ship repair yard in India before returning to Britain as engineering manager of the Clyde shipbuilders Alexander Stephen and Sons Ltd. In 1963 he went to Moscow, heading a delegation of shipbuilding technical experts.

Three Clyde yards—Stephen's, John Brown and Co. of Clyde-bank and Scott's Shipbuilding and Engineering Co. of Greenock—had agreed to act together when the Russians invited tenders for six mother factory ships. These were 30,000 tonners which would carry small purse seine netters slung on davits.

After a week in Moscow, the yards' principals had come home to say the Russians wanted specifications 'considerably altered' and in this confused situation the technical team flew to Moscow. With Bill Lochridge were two naval architects—David Watson from Stephen's, and Tom Savage from Scott's—and Graham Strachan, director of John Brown's engineering division.

During the negotiations they were invited into the office of one of the vice presidents of Sudoimport, the state purchasing company, and they noticed there a model of a vessel which looked like *Fairtry*.

David Watson told the vice president that Bill Lochridge had been with both *Fairtry* and *Fairfree*. The Russian rose and went to his bookcase, from which he took out the paper David Cunningham had read at the Paris fisheries congress and two presented by Bill Lochridge—one given to the Institution of Engineers and Shipbuilders in Scotland in 1950 about *Fairfree* and the other he had given to that body six years afterwards dealing with *Fairtry* and with other fishing developments.

"Lochridge?" he asked, "The same?"

Bill Lochridge had seen the Pushkin trawlers operate. While he was testing trawls for Sir Dennis' consortium he had stood on the deck of the Hellyer trawler *Benvolio* off Bear Island and had observed them for some time through powerful binoculars.

The Russians had had access to *Fairtry* plans, but they had no knowledge of how her stern trawling gear operations had been determined, and this was obvious as he watched.

"Yes," he said, and nodding towards the model, "I watched you trawling. You were a lot slower than *Fairtry* handling the gear. In 300 fathoms we could bring it in, empty the cod ends, make repairs and be fishing again in 35 minutes. Your ships took $1\frac{1}{2}$ hours."

Then he added, "She is just like *Fairtry*."

The remark was more question than statement, but the reply was non-commital.

"Ah," said the Russian, "but not 35 minutes."

His guest was too mindful of the importance of the orders the delegation sought to probe further.

The scenario could have been a re-run from ten years before. The Russians talked of needing three ships rather than six, and they also wanted to change their power to steam turbine. Though this was a radical turn-around, the delegation worked all night on new drawings. They were left as consolation with an order for just three fully-automated dredgers, to be built by Stephen's recently acquired subsidiary, Simons Lobnitz.

"One of the 30,000 tonners was built at Vladivostok," said Bill Lochridge. "I never did hear what happened about the others, but I've no doubt they used our designs. And these would be among the first of their giant size of mother ships."

The entry of the Russians' Pushkin on the scene did not deter Captain Harold from adding to his venture. At the end of *Fairtry*'s second year of operation she had made a trading profit of £100,000. When he built *Fairtry* he had wanted to order a companion for her. Now he went to the board to seek approval to build not just one but two more *Fairtrys*. Major Noel was opposed to ordering even one vessel, much less two, but Captain Harold won the argument, and in July, 1956, the board agreed—Noel still dissenting—to place an order for two vessels with Wm Simons of Renfrew.

No British trawler owner followed Captain Harold's lead in building.

Sir Dennis was of course unaware of the suspicious manner in which the Russians had copied *Fairtry*, but their espousal of the concept heightened his disappointment that in Britain only Salvesen had done so.

He blamed the innate conservatism of the industry (though conceding that a discouraging factor was Government grants and loan policy which disfavoured distant water vessels), and he wrote: "Like other inventions and developments in which the pioneering work has been done in Britain, the application on a major scale has been taken up by the foreign nations and Britain is allowing the fruits of its initiative to be gathered by others. . . .

"Russia has 24 *Fairtry* class trawlers and is now planning another 30, making a total of 54. Germany has placed contracts for one and is contemplating ten more. Spain is also in the market for another. The score is therefore foreign contracts placed and pending 65 to 70, Britain three."

Strictures from a source which could only be seen in the industry as biased made no impact on the trawler owners. An authoritative state such as Russia could build without regard to economic factors, they said; it was quite another matter for those in an industry which oft-times struggled. It was also yet to be proven valid to trawl from the stern, however that might be so, or was necessary, from a factory trawler.

The vessel which pointed a different way was the charter chosen in 1954 from John Bennett's Northern fleet to carry out the Torry freezing at sea experiment. *Northern Wave*, an 18 year old German-built steam-driven vessel, was typical of the bulk of the sidewinder fleet. If she could freeze at sea and bring back quality fish that sold, any other sidewinder similarly adapted with minimum design adjustment could do the same.

For nine months Torry's men sailed in her, cramped in a small hitherto unused cabin for'ard and living in times of storm on tinned sardines until in September 1956 the experiment was pronounced a success.

For John Bennett, who had managed *Northern Wave* throughout the experiment, its success justified the stance he had taken within his father's counsels as advocate of freezing at sea. As early as 1948 he had encouraged Bill Graham, his chief superintendent engineer, to draw up plans for a 200 foot diesel electric sidewinder capable of taking freezing equipment. At that time also he had met Dr George Reay, and they had become good friends.

He and his father determined in the light of the *Northern Wave* report to go further.

The Marr brothers meantime independently experimented with freezing plant ashore which they intended to install in one of their vessels, but among other owners there were few converts.

Fish was still in good demand despite that meat rationing had ended; it was also unclear whether it was economic to freeze at sea, and uncertainty prevailed over whether, if it was economic, they should convert sidewinders to freeze part of the catch as had been done with *Northern Wave*, or they should build, and if they built, whether they should trawl from the stern.

In this atmosphere of doubt Dr Reay asked a shipbuilder for a full-scale design, based on a sidewinder, which he could present to the hesitants.

CHAPTER EIGHT

A month after the decision to build two sisters for *Fairtry* the whaling company of Salvesen was taken into active participation in cold storage in Grimsby.

There were four public cold stores in the town.

Three belonged to Bill Bennett. They traded as Grimsby Cold Storage Ltd, a subsidiary of a company he formed in 1920 in London with David (later Sir David) Robertson, MP. He set up the first at Royal Dock in 1934 to hold his Greenland expedition cargoes, converted another from a warehouse a few hundred yards away, and a third from an old ice factory in East Robinson Street.

Odd store out in Grimsby was in Victor Street. It was the oldest in town, built in 1900 by the trawler owner Sir Alec Black originally to make ice for the fleet.

It was probably also odd store out in the whole of Britain, because no other was managed by a woman.

When Sir Alec's male staff had been called up one by one into the Armed Forces he had been dismayed to find his clerkess, Mrs Lillian Wells, intended to leave for a position with more money. He solved both his problems by doubling her salary and promoting her as manager. After his death the store was taken over by a consortium of merchants, and latterly by Union International, owned by the Vestey group, but still with Mrs Wells in charge.

Ted Sealey customarily sought space for *Fairtry*'s cargoes as soon as he learned that the vessel was headed homeward. Both Mrs Wells and the managers of Bennett's stores were pleased to have his custom but none of them could guarantee in advance that there would be room for the cargo of a ship which was at sea for at least two months and could return with a 500 or 600 ton load.

One day in August 1956 as *Fairtry* landed her catch all four stores were crammed with other people's goods, and Ted Sealey had to load the cargo into refrigerating lorries (of which there were not many to be had) and distribute parcels here and there all around the surrounding area.

They knew then that they would need a cold store of their own.

Salvesen had not the expertise to build. But once more when Max Harper Gow was in a difficulty Leslie Marr came to him with an offer, proposing that Salvesen join with him and his brother in a store they planned to build in Hull.

The only proviso he made was that Salvesen should not build another in competition in Hull; each was free otherwise to build elsewhere. Either at any time could take his departure if he wished; it was a working partnership holding out opportunities to learn from each other, and Max Harper Gow accepted readily.

The firm which the brothers sought as a straw company was Andrew Johnson Knudtson of Hull. The principal of it was John Willie (Johnny) Johnson, whose daughter Amy was famed as the pioneer girl pilot who in 1931 flew a second hand plane alone across three continents to Australia.

Leslie Marr was a friend of the family. He and Amy had been in the RAF Auxiliary during the war—he to survive, she to lose her life. When Leslie Marr asked Johnny Johnson to sell his company, his old friend agreed.

Marr took two thirds of the shares, Salvesen the rest.

To protect the catches of their three vessels, Salvesen availed themselves of the freedom to build outwith Hull, and a 3000 ton capacity store was planned in Grimsby's Levington Street. Ted Sealey was appointed to manage it.

At this point Bill Bennett began unexpectedly to discuss with Max Harper Gow a possible interest in the *Fairtrys* undertaking.

No doubt he was prompted by the £100,000 profit which *Fairtry* had made; a further lure may have been the projected cold store at Levington Street.

Informal talks went on sporadically for several months. During them, Max Harper Gow found himself with other responsibilities— Iver Salvesen died in September from a heart attack, and he and Gerald Elliot had to take charge of the merchant fleet.

The Associated's chairman in any case was too absorbed with other plans to himself wish to hasten negotiations; he was resolved to catch up with Birds Eye's lead in the frozen food business.

Birds Eye was claiming "an insatiable demand" for fish-fingers, the new market runaway; the cuckoo they had put into the Smethurst nest was taking up so much room that Unilever decided Birds Eye might as well take up the nest entirely, and in the subsequent merger Miss Swallow's fish cakes were gradually phased out.

In October Bill Bennett announced the merger of his three frozen foods companies as "Eskimo Foods Limited", and he accompanied the announcement with a challenge to the front runner.

"Eskimo," he said, "will become a household word."

He gave control of the three-in-one company—and the task of making his boast reality—to Joe Sprott and Mick Coburn, whom he had left since 1954 to develop independently of his other interests.

He arrived at Bernard Street office in Leith on Friday, 13 December, 1957, seeking "a form of partnership to integrate fish production and orthodox trawling and distribution of frozen food production."

Talks ranged from the formation of a joint company to operate the three ships, or to his taking over the Fresh Frozen Foods company in entirety, or to his chartering the vessels, or to his taking the ships in exchange for shares in Associated, valuing the vessels at just under £3 million.

Captain Harold's favoured outcome was an agreement that granted Bill Bennett bareboat charter with Salvesen retaining the management of the vessels, coupled with the issue of a considerable holding of Associated shares to Salvesen at an agreed price. He was careful in the negotiations to exclude the Levington Street store from any proposed deal.

But in that winter in which many storms assailed the fleets *Fairtry* no more than covered her costs. Bill Bennett's enthusiasm for a deal waned when he learned the year's results. The negotiations dragged and reached no promising stage.

Salvesen and Marr opened their joint store in Hull in February, 1958. Tom Summers, who became its secretary and latterly managing director, remembers the event coinciding with the disaster at

Munich airport when the plane carrying Manchester United's football team crashed and most of the famous 'Busby Babes' died. "And not surprisingly," he said, "the opening of a cold store did not merit attention in the local newspapers."

By the autumn of that year Bill Bennett had made no further move. Associated planned instead to build their own freezer trawler—and she would trawl from the stern as *Fairtry* did.

But Carl Ross came a-wooing.

While he had been a merchant he had always said his ambition was to be a trawler owner. Now the trawler owner wanted to be a force as formidable as—or more so than—his rivals Bill Bennett and Birds Eye.

After building his automated factory on South Quay a sprawl of buildings had followed along what became known as Ross Road.

Since taking Alex Alexander and his companies into his group in 1952, however, he looked beyond the confines of Grimsby and of the fish his vessels caught and in which he traded—he saw a greater profit to be reaped in the farmlands of East Anglia. But for the expansionary deals which he contemplated he needed much more capital than he and his directors could themselves muster.

He offered Salvesen a ten per cent stake in his group.

Although the offer was not tied directly to any deal over *Fairtry* fish, it represented a breakthrough in formerly stoutly-held bastions.

"There was an understanding that we would be mutually helpful on straightforward business terms and that we would help as much as possible in their marketing," said Carl Ross.

Salvesen accepted and Max Harper Gow joined the Ross board.

"We had decided he was the one we wanted," Carl Ross added. "The deal was important to us but I think it was important to them too, and that it aroused Max Harper Gow's interest in the frozen food business."

The association which began between Ross and Salvesen in September 1958 was to last until ten years later when the business which Carl Ross' father set up with a capital of £1200 was sold to the Imperial group for £44 million.

In August 1958 Ted Sealey's son Barry came down from

Cambridge with first class honours in Natural Science and he was invited by Max Harper Gow to join the company as a trainee manager. His duties were primarily to help to manage the *Fairtrys*, but for the first three months he helped his father to set up the new cold store in Levington Street. With all the brashness of his youth he called on Jim Dunlop, at that time assistant manager of Grimsby Cold Storage Ltd, and he borrowed stock sheets with which to establish procedures for his father's rival store.

Levington Street store opened in the winter of 1958. It was one of the first public stores in Europe laid out entirely as a store using pallets and forklift trucks. These were common in the United States, but in Britain everything that was delivered was unloaded from the lorries by hand on to little handcarts called 'dillies', then in turn unloaded in the chamber and laid on dunnage (pieces of wood supports which raised the products off the floor). Goods could then be built up in rows and blocked off at the ends.

There was a store manager, six storemen and a girl assistant. They had £10 petty cash and for several years invoicing work was done from head office in Leith.

The store had no engineer and the engines of the four large compressors frightened Ted Sealey at first. He said he "could not even ride a bicycle much less look after an engine." But when he voiced his fears to the engineers they said: "You don't have an engineer standing by your fridge at home, do you? Well, it's the same thing—only it's bigger."

The capacity of the store was greater than the three *Fairtrys* would fill at any one time, and it seemed sensible therefore to take in other people's goods.

There was little encouragement when the store opened for service. Ted Sealey offered a bottle of whisky as prize for the first customer and if the winner's three 14lb boxes of kippers looked pitifully forlorn in the large chamber, not much more followed at first to keep them company—mostly a few boxes which local curers delivered on the carriers of their bicycles.

At this time a new public store planned to be larger than any other was going up in the fields at Ladysmith Road.

Ladysmith Road was little more than a grassy lane, and the only occupants of what became a new industrial estate were the Birds Eye (formerly Smethurst) factory, and Bagueley's Transport and an ice rink in which for ten years Grimsby Redwings defied all other teams in Britain to topple them from their foremost place in ice hockey.

The new store was initiated by Helsingborg Fryshus AB, a cold storage company which had grown up with the quick freezing industry in Sweden and had the largest sub zero store in Europe. They called their British subsidiary Northern Cold Stores Ltd (later Frigoscandia). The managing director, Tore Lauritzson, built it primarily to serve the Scandinavian company Findus, which had been importing into Britain for three years and which planned to set up a factory in Grimsby.

Tore Lauritzson mistimed his venture. Though Birds Eye as well as Findus contracted to take space, he met only discouragement elsewhere, and, unable to sustain it financially, he allowed it to be known that he was prepared to take in partners or to sell.

Salvesen were interested. There was still the possibility of a deal with Associated, however, and concerned as he was to maintain good relations, Max Harper Gow gave Bill Bennett nine months to decide if he wanted to buy the store to add to the ones he already had.

The colossus of the fishing industry had just celebrated half a century in the business, feted by colleagues and by fellow leaders in the industry and presented with his portrait, painted by the distinguished artist Sir Frank Salisbury. But at this peak time in his career he was confronted with a family crisis. His son Peter unexpectedly announced he would resign from the company to follow a life in farming, and could not be dissuaded. His 66 year old father finally accepted failure and then himself took over Peter's charge of the group's distribution operations.

Whether this diverted his attention from a meeting with the Swedes, he waited until the nine months grace he had been given had almost elapsed before travelling to Sweden. On 17 July, 1959, he and his partner Sir David Robertson were dining with Tore Lauritzson in Helsingborg when he collapsed with a heart attack.

His death was a shock to his friends and his colleagues. His son

John recalls—"He had for many years joked that when he died it would be at a grand party when he was 84. But he lived hard and he did tempt fate a bit."

Associated's talks with the Swedes ended. The board was more urgently engaged in the reorganisation which the loss of their principal entailed. (John Bennett, who was appointed managing director, on finding himself not long afterwards facing a threatened takeover by Carl Ross, buttressed his defences by persuading the stores magnate Sir Hugh Fraser—Lord Fraser of Allander—to assume the chairmanship).

Bound no longer by his offer to Bill Bennett, Max Harper Gow opened negotiations with Tore Lauritzson.

At a dinner in Fishmongers' Hall in London he listened to a speech by James Parratt, successor to George Muddiman as chairman of Birds Eye. The boom in frozen food was on its way, said James Parratt, and the cold storage industry was not in a position to cope with it. If the operators failed to provide the cold storage that was needed, the processors would have to do it for themselves.

"No one paid much attention to that part of his speech except ourselves," said Max Harper Gow. "But here we were with the opportunity to do it in a substantial way with Northern Cold Stores. We had come into Ross as shareholders and we had learned from that and we were getting experience in cold storage. But when James Parratt made that speech it gave us confidence to go ahead with it as a main business."

On the verge of an accord with Tore Lauritzson he was freed of his greatest concern—Carl Ross offered to take all *Fairtry* fish.

The board had refused two such offers in the past, fearing exploitation by anyone with a monopoly of the catches, but as a minute recorded, the managers felt their connections with Ross would ensure fair dealings. The deal signed by Max Harper Gow, Carl Ross and Jack Vincent was said by Jack Vincent to be "the largest contract in the British fishing industry," and he pledged "full use of the group's distributive organisation."

Tore Lauritzson's store opened in August 1959, and two months later he accepted Salvesen's terms.

There was no immediate takeover, however; Tore Lauritzson's

venture having been partly financed with a Swedish state grant, if he sold within five years he was subject to heavy tax, and Salvesen agreed he should operate the store and control it until the five years had passed.

CHAPTER NINE

When Captain Harold Salvesen and Max Harper Gow decided to join with the British fishing fleet and its Navy escorts in the so-called First Cod War, a Cabinet Minister tried to stop them.

The events that led to confrontation with John Hugh Hare, the then Minister of Agriculture and Fisheries, trace back to the arrival of Loftur Juliusson for an interview in Max Harper Gow's office at the end of 1957.

Loftur Juliusson, aged 37, married, with a home in Reykjavik, was seeking a post as fishing skipper. He had been recommended by Gaer Zoega, head of Zoegatrawlers, who acted as agent for Salvesen in Iceland.

Gaer Zoega was not called upon often. In all *Fairtry*'s fifteen voyages she had never fished in Icelandic waters. The grounds were no more distant than a few days steaming, and the fish was of good quality, but hauls were less than in the far grounds where *Fairtry* found the volume she needed to sustain her. Irrespective also of the quality of the fish *Fairtry* might catch there, when it would be frozen it would fetch no premium price.

Leo Romyn and Jim Cheater had always advised they avoid Iceland. The notoriously rough and rocky ground there posed considerable risk of damage to expensive gear, since the powerful vessel often could not pull up in time if she encountered a snag.

When therefore during the interview Juliusson advanced the thought that his familiarity with the grounds could be used to extend *Fairtry*'s operations, the suggestion did not impress as he had hoped.

On the other hand, Max Harper Gow sorely needed competent skippers to join Leo Romyn and Jim Cheater when the two new *Fairtry* vessels would complete, and the convention that one did not

75

entice rivals' skippers restricted his recruitment to men of lower rank and aptitude.

Loftur Juliusson was a man of proven talent in his native fleet. His Icelandic certificate did not permit him to sail as master in a British vessel, but so long as a trawler carried a British certificated master and one mate with a certificate, she could carry an uncertificated second mate as a catcher. Max Harper Gow signed on Loftur Juliusson as 'Fishing Officer'.

Leo Romyn shared Max Harper Gow's doubts whether Juliusson's suggestion was of value, but he accepted that the Icelander's coming provided an opportunity to test the water, perhaps in season, by occasional hauls on the way to and from the far grounds.

In the midst of the long dispute between Britain and Iceland over limits there was, besides, peace—however uneasy, and perhaps more properly to be termed a truce.

Loftur Juliusson sailed with Leo Romyn as master and Jim Cheater as mate on *Fairtry*'s voyage No 16 in March, 1958. The quiet-mannered, friendly Icelander could have found the voyage disturbing, for the German mechanics on board voiced suspicion that he had been sent to spy on the vessel's operations before Iceland secured factory ships of her own, and his subsequent voyages might have been made more difficult had not Max Harper Gow acted promptly to dispel the rumour before it could cause harm.

In June Iceland ended the two year truce, declaring that whatever the outcome of the deliberations on limits by a United Nations' Conference on the Law of the Sea, she would impose a 12 mile limit around her coast to take effect on 1st September. Britain warned she would resist any attempt to keep out her fishermen.

A month after that declaration, Juliusson sailed again with Romyn and Cheater—again to the far grounds, but this time on the way out *Fairtry* fished off Iceland for the first time.

Perhaps if Leo Romyn had persevered the trial could have been less discouraging, but he could not afford the time and he continued his voyage westward.

At dawn on 1st September 1958, when Leo Romyn on the Grand Banks was close to filling and heading for home, more than a hundred vessels of the British fleet were crossing the disputed

76

twelve mile limit. In three packs, each protected by a naval frigate, they fished within boxes codenamed Spearmint, Butterscotch and Toffeeapple.

The Icelandic gunboat patrols did not interfere.

But next day the gunboats *Thor* and *Maria Julia* seized the Grimsby trawler *Northern Foam*—one of John Bennett's fleet—and tried to take her into Reykjavik, only to find that her crew had disabled the engines, and when HMS *Eastbourne* arrived and boarded with grappling irons, the Icelandic prize party found themselves taken as 'guests' on board the frigate.

The 'war' was then truly joined.

Leo Romyn passed by the 'battleground' with his holds full, and arrived at Immingham on 4 October.

From then he and Loftur Juliusson stood by *Fairtry 2* and Jim Cheater, who was scheduled to take *Fairtry 3*, assumed command of *Fairtry*.

Jim Cheater took *Fairtry* on her voyage No 18 from October 1958 until February 1959 and fished the distant grounds without going into Icelandic waters.

But in this time the Cod War had been escalating in incident; seven Icelandic gunboats prowled, ever harassing, sometimes ramming, seeking in period of mist or darkness to board the vessels of their unwelcome visitors, and foiled only by the constant vigilance of the trawlermen and their escorts' crews.

When *Fairtry 2* was making ready for her maiden voyage, Captain Harold and Max Harper Gow decided that as their vessels voyaged to and from their customary grounds they should demonstrate solidarity with the beset British fleet.

Leo Romyn, too, was concerned to identify with the old comrades with whom he had sailed out of Hull.

"We never supposed other than that our appearance among the fleet would have been welcome," said Max Harper Gow.

But when the Ministry of Agriculture and Fisheries learned of their voyage plans, a senior official telephoned. His Minister, so he informed Max Harper Gow, would prefer a factory ship did not enter Icelandic waters.

Pressed to say why, the aide said his Minister considered that a vessel as large as *Fairtry* would be 'added provocation to the Icelanders', and he asked for an assurance that his Minister's wishes would be respected.

Max Harper Gow was surprised and disturbed.

"We were being asked to break a well-established practice in fishing," he said, "that once the areas of operation in voyage plans had been discussed between owner and skipper, the skipper was free to use his discretion to fish wherever it was legal to do so. If I were to tell Leo Romyn he could not support his fellow fishermen, and order him not to fish where we had already agreed, I would need very good reason to do so, and the reason I had been given seemed bizarre to say the least.

"It was obvious the Ministry official expected my immediate compliance. I told him instead I could give him no assurance. He telephoned back later to say the Minister desired me to come to London to see him."

When Max Harper Gow consulted with Captain Harold, the chairman's surprise was as great as had been that of his young colleague. He decided he would himself see the Minister.

"Captain Harold didn't like bureaucratic interference," said Max Harper Gow. "He had been fighting it all his working life. He thought I was standing up for a fishing principle. But he was a fair-minded man, and he was quite prepared to discuss the request— or was it an order?—and if there was a case, say, involving the national interest, we would comply."

John Hugh Hare, who later became Lord Blakenham in the administration headed by Edward Heath, had transferred some months before from the Ministry of War.

There was no marriage of minds at the meeting in London. Captain Harold had gone prepared to listen and to take account of any circumstances, perhaps that might be seen as compromising solution of the dispute. "But there was no hint of that," said Max Harper Gow, "no reason other than what I had been already given. The Minister simply repeated his thinly-veiled order. Captain Harold was furious, and when he came back he told me: 'We go ahead'."

Jim Cheater sailed *Fairtry* on her voyage No 19 on 19 March, 1959. He carried a spare deckhand; Barry Sealey was conforming

78

with Captain Harold's requirement that all aspiring to management should learn by practical experience every aspect of what they would manage. His learning extended to mending nets, splicing wires, gutting fish, steering and tending machines in the factory.

Fairtry fished off Vestmannaeyjar Island from 23 March without interference from the Icelandic patrols but with such disappointing result that Barry Sealey in a letter later wrote: "It seems from our present experience . . . we could never make a fortune from our ships fishing in Icelandic waters"—and at the end of 18 days Cheater was lured away to join a concentration of vessels feeding on a goodly find of haddock on the Grand Bank off St Pierre Island.

Fairtry 2 was ready by that time. She and her sister were basically the same as *Fairtry* but were electrically driven, and bigger, with more factory space and storage space and with accommodation for a crew of 96—ten more men than *Fairtry*.

Salvesen published their plans for all to know. There was nothing left to conceal; the damage had already been done.

Leo Romyn took *Fairtry 2* on her maiden voyage on 1st April. Characteristically, he delayed casting off until 96 Bibles which he had ordered and had not arrived were rushed by taxi to the quayside.

Not only Bibles had been missing, however. He had no flags ("No Code of International Signals, not even an Ensign," he complained later). The lack of a Red Ensign was to be more embarrassing than he might have realised.

From the start of the voyage he was less than happy with his new vessel. Excessive vibration caused many pipe breakages in the engine room, and it was 7 April before he arrived off the southwest coast of Iceland and began to fish while his chief engineer sought to repair the damages.

On 10 April he was radioing urgently for spares to be sent by a trawler bound for the grounds, or by the Navy's mailboat. There was no way this could have been done without embarrassing other vessels at the grounds, and when he was told this, he asked for the spares to be sent instead to St John's. Hauls moreover had been poor, and, he said, "reports from French and Portuguese ships at Newfoundland are such we cannot afford to remain here."

The two *Fairtrys* met on the Grand Banks and Barry Sealey was transferred to the new vessel, crossing in a dory "amid waves so high that in the troughs I couldn't see either ship," he recalled, and being hoisted on board in a sling.

On the way home two months later Leo re-entered Iceland's waters. On 8 July he was fishing off Grimsey Island on the northern coast when the gunboat *Thor* challenged him.

The Reykjavik newspaper *Althydubladid* reported the arrival of *Fairtry 2* as 'New Guest among British Poachers', and it carried a photograph, taken by one of *Thor*'s crew, captioned 'The Ship More Splendid Than Her Business'.

If the paper thought it surprising to find Icelander Loftur Juliusson on board 'on the wrong side', as it were, it noted his presence without comment. It reported *Fairtry 2* as fishing illegally four miles inside the fishing limit, "and in addition in an illegal condition in that she flew no flag."

The report continued: "Immediately *Thor* pulled alongside the trawler the warship *Duncan* arrived with Commodore Anderson on board. The *Thor* drew attention to the fact that the trawler had no flag and that investigation must be made as to her nationality, for this might be a Russian or a French trawler. The British then immediately admitted nationality and remedied the flag deficiency by borrowing a flag from another British trawler."

Next day, said the newspaper, *Fairtry* was "still fishing illegally six to seven nautical miles inside the limit" off Grimsey Island.

"The captain of the *Thor* exchanged words with the skipper of the trawler and pointed out to him that he was fishing illegally. The skipper replied: 'Can you tell me in which other place fish is to be had?'"

Leo Romyn's irony was lost on Captain Eirikur Kristofersson, who replied that 'it was not his duty to point out fishing grounds to British poachers'.

Had Captain Kristofersson returned the following day he would have found Leo Romyn still fishing 'illegally' a little further to the eastward.

He was by then short of food, radioing for 400 lbs of flour and 140 lbs of sugar to be sent by a trawler bound for Iceland.

Five days later, having arranged rendezvous with the trawler carrying his food supplies, he headed home.

The week he had spent in Iceland's waters had been unrewarding.

"We had wanted to find out with Loftur Juliusson whether we could fish Iceland, but we soon learned there was little likelihood of our making anything of it," said Max Harper Gow. "And of course our incursions into the grounds latterly were intended mainly as a gesture of identification with the British fleet's cause."

The First Cod War went on for two years afterwards (and ended on Iceland's terms) but the *Fairtrys* took no further part.

CHAPTER TEN

By contrast to the disappointing foray in Icelandic waters, the distant grounds of Newfoundland and Greenland gave catches as bountiful as before, such that after *Fairtry 3* joined in February 1963 at least one, and sometimes two, vessels came back heavily laden every month.

Barry Sealey, who by then had been appointed Max Harper Gow's personal assistant (but still with attention to the *Fairtrys* as his primary duty) was commuting from Leith to meet them, and he had to carefully arrange the date of his wedding with fiancée Helen to avoid clashing with the homecoming of any one of them.

But there was soon justification of the cautionary note which Max Harper Gow had sounded at the trials of *Fairtry 2*:

"Providing that all the trawlers operating in northern waters adhere to mesh regulations," (of the international fishing commissions) "there should be sufficient fish for all for the foreseeable future.

"However, the large increase in Russian and other trawlers is bound to result in a good year group being fished up quicker than before, so I suppose we cannot expect so many good years as we have had in the past. If we get two or three reasonably good fishing years out of seven, I think we shall have to be satisfied."

By the summer of 1960 the invasion of the North Atlantic had already assumed proportion to cause alarm, Leo Romyn reporting from *Fairtry 2* while off the coast of Labrador that there were at least 200 Russian and Polish ships, which—so the directors ruefully noted—"were not so much concerned with observance of mesh regulations and other conservation measures."

Throughout that year more foreigners came. It was taking the *Fairtrys* so much longer to fill their holds that Salvesen embarked

82

on a unique experiment. The 550 ton *Ross Hunter* was chartered to accompany *Fairtry 2*, feeding the mother ship throughout a voyage longer than any undertaken before by a sidetrawler.

The *Ross Hunter* carried fuel to last two months, and was scheduled to bunker at St John's when this was exhausted. Since she would have no fish in her holds, she took no crushed ice, and carried sandbags as ballast.

Barry Sealey, who had never sailed in a vessel so small, joined the 20 men who volunteered to crew her.

She left on New Year's Eve, 1960, sailing into seas that snapped thick pound boards like matchsticks, and she wallowed alarmingly all the way over the Atlantic.

Fairtry 2 did not stop her own fishing to accommodate her urchin. *Ross Hunter*'s catches were transferred in large detachable cod ends, strung together on a long nylon line and streamed from a side gate with a buoy. *Fairtry 2* then steamed up, shackled on to the line, and hauled the catch over her ramp on to the deck.

In varying weather every day this went on until 3300 baskets of fish, weighing 100 tons, had passed to the 'mother' by the end of the two-month long voyage. But while it had been proved a practicable proposition, the catch was not thought sufficient to justify repeating.

The fish-finger block market which might have brought them good return was also yielding little. By taking out the pin bones by hand at sea they were producing an average of 60 to 70 tons each voyage; although on one trip when Barry Sealey acted as factory manager 160 tons of fish-finger blocks were landed out of a total 600 tons, this was an exception.

"Woe betide us too if any little bones were left in," said Max Harper Gow. "We never did succeed in doing it mechanically, and we had to go on depending on the catering trade."

In August 1961 the retired *Fairfree*, after lying at The Shore at Leith for ten years and becoming almost a landmark there, was towed out to be broken up at Inverkeithing. The only mourner at her funeral noted by the local newspaper was a girl who threw a bouquet of flowers into the water as the old ship passed through the swing bridge. (The newspaper report left the reader to speculate as to her identity or as to why she did it.)

In the same month in which the old prototype ended her existence, the trawler *Lord Nelson*, first stern-trawling freezer built for a British trawler owner, was coming back from a maiden voyage of 36 days with a near-record haul for her home port of Hull.

Apart from the fact that she trawled from the stern and as consequence was ordered from a German yard reputed to have acquired particular expertise in that design form, *Lord Nelson*, which was 238 feet in length and 1200 tons gross, was a natural progression from the *Northern Wave* experiment. She was a part freezer, following on a larger scale the Torry freezer layout, and Gordon Eddie and Torry engineering colleagues supervised installation of her 16 six-station freezers.

Described by A. C. Hardy as "a halfway house . . . a cautious but clearly-worked out probe into the future," the trawler which Bill Bennett planned before his death was sent into Tom Boyd's Lord Line.

Another stern trawling freezer, built by Leslie and Geoffrey Marr, followed a year later.

Theirs was the first in the fleet to freeze *all* her catch. She was 240 feet in length and 1435 tons gross, and carried eleven 12-station freezers. She was the product of four years of experiments; before ordering her from Hall Russell's yard in Aberdeen the brothers had developed a freezer on shore, then converted the sidetrawler *Marbella* to take a one-station freezer, and had followed that by converting the sidetrawler *Junella* to take two six-station freezers.

The brothers renamed the sidewinder so that they could give the name *Junella* to the new vessel.

Leslie Marr was seriously ill then, though still taking active part in the business. When he asked Leo Romyn to take command of *Junella*, Leo rejoined his old employer. 'Skipper' had promised Max Harper Gow he would stay with *Fairtry* for a year; he had stayed instead for eight, and made what was to prove a life-long friendship with his 'Gaffer'.

Junella was launched in March 1962—with her wheelhouse deckhead heightened to a foot above normal so that Leo Romyn could stand in the wheelhouse in comfort.

Both *Junella* and *Lord Nelson* froze only whole fish, were smaller than *Fairtrys*, fished less time at sea, and carried only 20 to 25 crew.

In the years after the arrival of these two vessels, new building in Britain's distant water fleet would all freeze in some form or another and would trawl from the stern. But in 1962 other nations were building in no penny numbers as the British were doing. Bulgarian, East German and Spanish stern trawling freezers and factory ships were arriving to proliferate the Atlantic swarm.

Even for Jim Cheater, whom they called 'Lucky Jim', there were few places to hide from his rivals.

Ted Younge was with *Fairtry 2* on one voyage when she located a shoal. In earlier days he had seen no other deepsea trawler on the Grand Banks and there was none in sight when *Fairtry 2* began to take in her find. He went to his bunk for the night and woke next morning to find to his astonishment 40 vessels fishing around her.

In March 1962 Captain Harold had to report to his shareholders that conditions were "very difficult", and he added "we are seriously considering redeployment or disposal of the fleet."

"By that time, of course," said Max Harper Gow, "we had done the deal with Tore Lauritzson to take his cold store and our eyes were on cold storage as the possible successor."

The board decided to try to find a buyer for the original *Fairtry*. But in October, when the board met on the motion of Major Noel to discuss 'future fishing policy', it was reported that negotiations with a prospective buyer in the Eastern European bloc gave no indication of a reasonable price for the vessel. The board accepted the venture had not been a financial success "and when assessing current capital values part of the original costs have to be regarded as permanently lost. . . ."

Without a buyer, *Fairtry* perforce continued to endure with her sisters as long as possible in the ever-more difficult market.

By 1963 the managers were reporting voyages having to last even longer, and "increased competition from factory trawlers of all the nations."

The 'increased competition' included for the first time the Japanese.

"We fear," said the managers' report, "their effort may increase substantially, further depleting the stocks which are already suffering from the high level of fishing effort."

The entry of the Japanese fishing fleet into the North Atlantic came, ironically, at the same time that Salvesen was finally giving up the Antarctic whaling grounds to their Japanese and Russian rivals.

CHAPTER ELEVEN

Five hundred men, remnants of a force which in its heyday mustered more than 2000, came home from Antarctica in 1963.

Many had gone whaling all their working lives, as their fathers before them. They had become conditioned to the ending; the writing on the wall which Captain Harold had spelled out when it was no more than a smudge had become starkly clear in the latter years for everyone to see.

His fears had begun to be realised five years before.

In 1958 the Whaling Commission set a catch limit of 15,000 units. Within this limit the five Antarctic nations agreed to negotiate quotas instead of competing in the free-for-all which had applied till then.

The intention was to continue to bring down this total catch limit to a level that the stocks could bear, each country organising its industry in line with its quota of the reduced catch.

This was a concept Captain Harold had urged for many years. But his relief was short-lived. The nations could not agree what the share of each should be, and the longer they argued the fewer stocks were left for them to argue over.

The subsidised Russian fleet could go on regardless of economic criteria—and, so it was held, without scruple for rules—as could also the low-paid Japanese fleet with a buoyant home market. But others could not.

Each Salvesen expedition, however as efficient as its rivals, was averaging a loss of about £100,000.

The Board saw the final run down of its whaling operations coming close—though everyone hoped that to lessen hardship for their crews they would be able to do this gradually over several seasons.

At this time Captain Harold decided to leave Max Harper Gow and Gerald Elliot to manage the company. When he conveyed his intention to the shareholders he told them: "I feel it is time for me to transfer my responsibilities to younger hands."

The partnership of Christian Salvesen and Co was dissolved at the end of 1960 and re-formed as Christian Salvesen and Co Ltd, with Max Harper Gow as its chairman and managing director. Gerald Elliot, for whom the expedition of 1958/59 was the last he engaged in, became assistant managing director.

The two were still able to avail themselves of Harold's wise counsel, for he remained as chairman of the owning South Georgia Co Ltd, but otherwise he devoted himself tirelessly to securing the best possible outcome of the international negotiations, taking part in conference after conference.

No one on the Board expected other than that the withdrawal would be not only emotionally painful but costly besides. However, it was established that no expedition could be sold without its quota, and these suddenly became valuable bargaining counters.

The Japanese were in the market for the sake of the quotas to be assigned to the expeditions, and the British, Norwegians and Dutch went into negotiations with them.

The first factory ship to go to the Japanese was Hector Whaling's *Balaena*.

Southern Venturer was to have been laid up in the season of 1960/61 but this plan was dropped, partly because *Balaena*'s sale made available Per Virik, one of the most successful whaling managers, and she and *Southern Harvester* both sailed, bolstered by the recruitment of Captain Virik and by several former *Balaena* catchers.

In the autumn of 1961 the Japanese bought *Southern Venturer* for £2,150,000. But since her sale did not call for delivery before June of 1962 she was able to set out on her 17th—and last— expedition.

Her sale, however, meant that retention of Leith Harbour as a repair base could no longer be justified.

At the end of that season of 1961/62 the two expeditions brought back with them every spare catcher at Leith Harbour they adjudged fit to survive the 7000 mile voyage home, manning them with volunteers from among the expeditions. Some who took duty on the bridge as officers of the watch had no certificates but were granted dispensation by the island's administrative officer.

Other catchers left at the base were securely moored against winter storms, while a few diagnosed as terminally ill were cannibalised for spare parts and then scuttled in the bay.

The catchers ended their voyage at Melsomvik, near Tønsberg, some to be prepared there for the following season, others to be laid up.

Southern Venturer discharged at Liverpool, was handed over to the Japanese and sailed at once to Japan, never to put to sea thereafter; her purchasers laid her up and later sent her to a scrapyard.

In 1962 the Antarctic nations finally reached agreement over quotas, and Captain Harold, as sole British survivor, secured entitlement to nine per cent of the total catch, allotted as four per cent to *Southern Venturer* on her sale to Japan, leaving five per cent for *Southern Harvester*.

Leith Harbour had not been totally abandoned, and Captain Harold Myhre from *Southern Venturer* took a squad of 30 there to attend to fuelling and other needs of the remaining floating expedition.

Southern Harvester sailed in the autumn of 1962, taking with her nine of the best catchers. The expedition formed a force described as "the most powerful in size and horse power the company has ever mounted," but everyone feared that the voyage might well be the last the *Harvester* would make.

There were no farewell parties—not even a wake—at the end of the 1962/63 season; a five-year long leave-taking had been too protracted for that.

When the expedition was ready to sail home, and *Southern Lotus*, which had been disabled at the end of the season, had been shackled to a towrope from the stern of a companion catcher; when the last moveable item of value had been shipped out in barges to the factory ship, and when all was battened down, *Southern Harvester*'s motor boat still waited at the base.

William (Bill) Lynch, secretary/storekeeper, was still on shore.

Bill Lynch had been a whaler since soon after the end of the War. A Londoner (this a rare species in his chosen working world) he married a nurse from the Shetlands while both were in the Army, and followed her to her home town, there to come to regard himself as one with the islanders.

"Leith Harbour was home to me for part of the year for 13 years," he said. "It was like a small town, day and night lights in the houses and works, chimneys smoking, steam hissing, always noise. Now it was silent, like a ghost town in the movies."

He should have hurried; Captain Virik on *Harvester* was impatient to be under way. But he walked out of the deserted station to Gun Point, where Red Laurenson and his men had manned puny defence against raiders who never came to give them cause to fire a shot in anger. It overlooked the bay and had been his favourite walk. When he eventually climbed the jacob's ladder to *Harvester*'s deck, he stayed there until the vessel passed the Black Rocks at the entrance to the bay "and I never thought I would see it again," he said.

The vessels arrived back without mishap to the lame duck *Southern Lotus*, though not without concern for her through the Roaring Forties; the Japanese bought *Southern Harvester* and took a three year lease of Leith Harbour, and with that there ended not only a half century of Salvesen tradition but a Scottish heritage which began when Charles I licensed the first Scots adventurers and the ships of Leith and Dundee and Peterhead sailed to hunt in the Arctic.

Most of the whalers were Norwegians and Scots, the latter mainly from the Shetlands and the Outer Isles. For the comparatively few who did not find other work a hardship fund was set up to aid their re-settlement. Gerald Elliot, who had kept them informed throughout the rundown, wrote: "One of the saddest aspects of giving up our whaling activities has been that we have had to part with so many good companions on both sides of the North Sea whose experience and steadfastness has supported us in the hazards of these ventures."

Bill Lynch, who had thought he would never see South Georgia again, *did* go back to Leith Harbour.

He and Captain William Johansen volunteered to go as liaison officers to help the Japanese run the land station and they took five technicians with them.

But after two years' tenancy the Japanese repented of their bargain, paid and gave up, and one sunny day they and the little British group went round the station greasing all machinery, opening valves and blowing pipes and laying corrugated iron sheets over windows before joining the Japanese transport *Mitsushima Maru*, which waited, dressed with flags and bunting, in the bay. On her deck the hosts and their guests drank toasts in saki to the British, the Norwegians, the Japanese, to Leith Harbour, and Strømness Bay and South Georgia, and to the whaling inspectors and to whomever and whatever else that they could think of.

In the years afterwards the remnants of the catching fleet would sink at their moorings under the burden of snow on their decks, or be dashed to pieces on shore in storm, and the station would crumble. Except for occasional calls by meteorologists and other scientists, and inquisitive Russians, and once by a television crew, it would remain deserted and desolate until an Argentinian military junta would misguidedly decide to invade the Falklands. . . .

Captain Harold now bowed out, as he had determined to do when he began the rundown.

He was 66 years old; if he felt his health to be failing, certainly no one suspected it, but he told Max Harper Gow he would give up the chair of the parent company and propose him as his successor at the next annual meeting of shareholders. Max Harper Gow had just succeeded to the vice chairmanship upon the retiral of Major Noel, and had not expected to follow Captain Harold so soon in the chair.

"He had an absolute obsession about not becoming a tiresome old man, but he was not going to give up until he knew his succession was in sound hands," said Max Harper Gow. "At some stage he must have decided Gerald and I could cope, and having got rid of the whaling fleet we two should carry on with his blessing."

Captain Harold had taken no personal part in the negotiations with the Japanese.

Southern Harvester had given less return than *Venturer* because by the time of her sale whale stocks had fallen so low that the overall limit was cut to 10,000 units, leaving her share little more than 500. The Japanese paid no more than £1,050,000 and they made a proviso that Salvesen buy her back at the end of her three year quota for £600,000.

Even so, the two factory ships had fetched about £2 million more than they were worth to anyone not engaged in whaling, and when Captain Harold learned the final outcome of the deals he gleefully told his personal assistant Tod Bell Scott, "That's jam on the cake!"

The 'cake' he left to his successors was itself substantial. Throughout the years the erstwhile tutor in economics had invested the surplus from whaling wisely and there was plenty of money for Max Harper Gow and Gerald Elliot to use.

The problem was how to convert it into business.

The merchant fleet and agencies run by Iver until his death in 1957, was the only sizeable former business, and they had continued his plans to modernise it. Some of the money now become available was used to build up the fleet further, but with vessels being laid up all over the world, they made no concerted effort to diverge into commercial shipping to an extent comparable with that undertaken by their old Norwegian whaling rivals.

A little capital was also diverted into building on land, firstly, with the intention of creating shopping centres and then turning to housebuilding, but at the time this was no more than an opportunist venture, promising little.

From the time the group had been formed, Gerald Elliot, however, had looked for other fishing opportunities, exhaustively studying conditions and techniques all over the world, and he led them into industrial fishing, that is, the deliberate catching of fish to convert it in plants ashore into meal and oil. The choice was logical; during the four seasons in which he had been in the Antarctic he had acquired considerable expertise in the reduction of whalemeat into oil and meal at Leith Harbour—an operation akin to what was done in fishmeal plants—and of course they were already familiar with the processes in limited form on board the *Fairtrys*.

Max Harper Gow also sent Barry Sealey to Grimsby to take advantage of a generous offer by Tore Lauritzson to give access to his store and all its operations six months before the due date of takeover.

Barry Sealey promptly decided that the potential of the cold storage business required that instead of commuting he should find a more permanent residence in the town.

His assessment of the potential was not misplaced. The store was in fact so lucrative that Tore Lauritzson hoped to come to some arrangement to keep a part in it, and at a farewell party which he gave to his customers on New Year's Eve of 1964 at the Flamingo Club in Humberston (with a young comedian named Bob Monkhouse to entertain the guests and strong Swedish 'glug' to warm them) he renewed hints that he would not be averse to the association continuing.

His hints were ignored, and on 1st January 1965 the Salvesen house flag was hoisted over the cold store, which became the headquarters of a new Grimsby subsidiary company set up to operate the cold stores and the three *Fairtrys*.

Barry Sealey was appointed its managing director, while his father took over day to day management of the two cold stores for him.

CHAPTER TWELVE

The *Fairtrys* within Barry Sealey's purview were even more beleaguered than before.

In what had been the pioneer's once lonely province the Russians hunted in packs, and huge as *Fairtry* had seemed compared with the trawlers of her day, she and her sisters were dwarfed by the company they were forced to keep.

After the Pushkin clone came larger and more sophisticated vessels, some equipped with hydro acoustic instruments able to locate fish at depths of 500 fathoms and over a radius of two miles. They spilled out into other oceans. Nowhere became too remote for the armadas which the major fishing nations built in the wake of *Fairtry*.

The United Nations' Food and Agriculture Organisation, which was exploring the resources of the seas scientifically and was stimulating development in backward countries to assuage the world's famine, was dismayed to find the big fleet nations were less concerned with its parallel campaign to harvest the resources rationally.

As the scramble increased, Roy Jackson, assistant director of fisheries of the organisation, was quoted as likening it to the Alaskan gold rush—"Who owns the stakes is unclear," he said (a reference to the dispute over limits), "it all depends who gets there first with the biggest shovel."

Gerald Elliot's incursion into industrial fishing began with a plant and fleet of anchoveta fishing boats which Salvesen and Peruvian partners took over in Peru, and thereafter he set out on a worldwide search for other opportunities.

Amid his prospecting in industrial fishing no outlet presented itself that might have given expectation also to use *Fairtrys*.

94

Prospects for these vessels in the Atlantic were dwindling fast. Their home market place became as crowded as the seas they fished. Nineteen freezers were together landing 50,000 tons a year of frozen cod to be thawed on shore and sold as fresh, and Norwegians and Germans were landing too. Prices slumped.

Fairtry could have been laid up had it not been feared that a breakdown by one of the other vessels would have endangered the contract with the Ross group.

Association with the enterprising and ambitious head of that group had been mutually advantageous.

In the years since Salvesen took a stake in his company, Carl Ross had acquired an importance in the frozen food business as considerable as he had in fishing. "We are no longer a trawling firm," he declared. "We are a processing company."

The local newspaper called him 'The Man With the Midas Touch'. His deals gave him a near-stranglehold on the potato market of East Anglia, a poultry business which he could boast as "the largest in Europe", a chain of vegetable and fruit shops, a supermarket, and a bridge restaurant, cafes and garage complex on the new M1 motorway. On a corner of one of the access roads to Grimsby docks he had opened in April 1964 a lofty headquarters the eleventh floor of which took the form of a trawler bridge. As 'Ross House' this tangible testimony to his power dominated Grimsby's skyline.

Not only was he taking all *Fairtrys'* fish but he was giving substantial business as well to the two cold stores Barry Sealey had taken over.

Ironically, when his executives began to complain of "serious difficulties in selling *Fairtry* fish" and of losing money on the sale, Barry Sealey was building another cold store over the town boundary in Cleethorpes to take care of all the Ross group's bulk storage in the Grimsby area.

The demands of that business on Barry Sealey's time dictated that someone else manage the *Fairtrys* for him, and A. H. (Tony) Hudson, who had been managing the Ross fleet, was appointed.

Voyages were then lasting almost five months, causing the ships to be difficult to man.

Willie Greenfield, the once-teenager of the first post-war whaling expedition, whose career thereafter had alternated between the expeditions and duties at head office crew department, was about to sail in the expedition of 1958/9 as secretary of *Southern Venturer* when he was recalled because of an emergency in the department. Among the responsibilities then given to him was the crewing of *Fairtrys*, and he tried to infiltrate several of the displaced whalers. But the experiment was not a success. Few took kindly to the change. Customs and attitudes differed, and the whalers found it difficult to relate to the fishermen, as did the fishermen to them.

Despite it having been accepted that *Fairtrys* were not a financial success, Salvesen were reluctant to quit the deep sea battleground, and in 1966 they asked Yarrow research department what should be the optimum size of freezer trawler. Had they built on the researchers' advice, they would have built smaller, as Associated and Marr had done, rather than larger as had their foreign imitators. But the board decided—"At the present time even such a vessel does not seem to offer sufficient return to justify building. As far as we can determine, there is no likelihood that any better results could be obtained by operating whole fish freezers as the other major trawler owners are doing."

Tony Hudson reduced the crew to 58. Not only were crews weary of spending so long a time on voyages; even their senior skipper Jim Cheater decided five months was too long for him too, and he left to join another company.

Costs escalated. When they reached £700 a day for each vessel Tony Hudson cut the average time away to a maximum of 16 weeks, scheduling only one bunker stop.

But just as they thought they had begun to stem the drain and to break even, the price of cod plummeted further.

Losses could no longer be sustained. The Atlantic would have to be abandoned.

Fairtry 3 was the first to be laid up. After completing a voyage in the spring of 1967 she sailed to Tønsberg. By coincidence, Hellyer were then sending *Coriolanus*, their first factory ship (or filleter as the Humber men called factory ships) out of Hull on her maiden trip. But managing director Mark Hellyer said he made "no certain predictions of success. A ship of the future, she will have to work in the confused present of the British trawling industry."

At this low tide in *Fairtrys*' affairs, 'Skipper' answered a call to help.

Within a year of his having agreed to go back to Leslie Marr, his old employer had died. Leo stayed two more years and then took part in Gerald Elliot's search for further fishing prospects. He was 65 when Tony Hudson persuaded him to assume command on a voyage in re-engined *Fairtry 2*.

That his skills were no less than before was evidenced when the vessel, which had lost money on her previous voyage, returned a good profit.

On Leo's next voyage *Fairtry 2* was almost lost; re-engined as she was, she broke down in a force 10 storm and she recovered power just in time to allow him to claw off a bleak and fearsome Greenland shore.

The veteran skipper left her in the Humber and did not go with her when she was withdrawn and she sailed to be laid up alongside *Fairtry 3* at Tønsberg.

Fairtry followed, carrying among her crew on that last trip chief engineer Jim Campbell and 2nd engineer Johnny Adams, who had been on her maiden voyage 13 years before and had served on her predecessor *Fairfree*.

Barry Sealey's announcement of the vessels' withdrawal included a hope that they could be made operational again 'if the situation improves'. But there was little likelihood of an improving situation in the Atlantic, and six hundred companies were informed that the *Fairtrys* were for sale or for charter.

Scarcely had *Fairtry 2* and *Fairtry 3* tied up than agents of Fidel Castro's Communist government arrived to inspect them. The Cubans were being trained by the Russians, and they already had 40 new vessels on order, but they were in the market to buy second hand as they awaited deliveries. Haste did not impel them, however, to take either vessel, even at reduced price.

Throughout that year and into 1968 propositions could have taken any one of the vessels to fish off the coasts of South America, or India, or Australia, or to be run jointly under the Norwegian flag, or—this last in conjunction with the White Fish Authority—to act as an experimental mother ship in the Atlantic. All these propositions came to nothing.

In the autumn of 1968 Tony Hudson flew to South Africa to try to interest someone in the vessels.

The White Fish Authority in this period was seeking new grounds for the distant water fleet's freezers—the trawlermen might not accept loss of traditional cod grounds as inevitable, but the Authority was more realistically looking at alternative sources which could be exploited. One such was the hake that the Russians had found in abundance six years before off the Cape of Good Hope.

At the end of a two year investigation, the Authority chartered the Marr trawler *Kirkella* to take scientists there for a final survey. The round trip of 11,800 miles was the first official British expedition outside traditional waters.

When upon her return Tony Hudson went to the Cape, he found a mammoth free-for-all. Ships of a dozen nations had joined the Russians.

Among them were two 20,000 ton ships familiar to whalers, operating under South African registry. One was the former Dutch whaling factory ship *Willem Barendzs*. The other was the *Suiderkreuz*—when she was built for the Norwegian fleet she had been named *Kosmos V*. Both vessels had been bought and converted by their new owners as floating fish meal factories to harvest the large pilchard stocks found off the coast.

In their first full season they gobbled up such an astonishing total of raw fish as to cause frenetic inshore men to label them "scourge" and "rapists of the ocean" and "plunderers", and to impel the government of South Africa and of its mandated territory South West Africa towards action against them.

There was no deal for Tony Hudson at the Cape, and in November 1968 the pioneer *Fairtry* was sold to the KM Corporation. Tony Hudson went back to Ross Trawlers.

Max Harper Gow reported to his shareholders "a disappointing end to a bold and imaginative enterprise."

Fairtry's remaining sisters continued to languish in Tønsberg while shipyards all over the world built vessels more capable and sophisticated than they. One of them eventually had to be scrapped— *Fairtry 3*, the younger and less reliable mechanically, went in July 1970 to a breaker's yard in Blyth, where her scrap fetched £42,250— and although there was no longer a role for *Fairtry 2* in the changed fishing scene, she found a more honourable fate, converted by her new owners, Vickers Oceanics Ltd, as a mother ship for mini submarines.

By that time there were as many as a thousand stern trawling freezers and factory trawlers of more than 1000 tons in the oceans of the world. The British, late converts as they were, had 37 stern trawling freezers and more planned. They included four factory trawlers—the big filleter *Coriolanus* and three mini versions of *Fairtry*, built by the Ranger company of North Shields.

Fairtry had brought about a fishing revolution.

Only a stranger to fishing could have formed the idea of her. Only an incomer bold as Captain Harold was could have adopted the concept and built a vessel which owed nothing to precedent or to accepted conventions.

But the words of Sir Andrew Lewis proved true—"It is a case of being first to venture and you know the pioneer inevitably loses money."

Fairtry and her sisters were a commercial failure. She was a ship ahead of her time. Not too far for those nations with little or no fishing past. But too far ahead to be welcome amid the fleet of her own country.

In any analysis, however, the British trawler owners cannot be said to have contributed to her failure. Though many did not wish her well, they all came to accept through the years she operated that Salvesen presented no threat to them, and the friendships which Max Harper Gow had with John Bennett and Tom Boyd and those he made with the Marr family and others have continued to the present day.

Salvesen was forced to rely on the catering trade. No inroad in retail was achieved because discolouration of fillets of fish frozen immediately at sea was never overcome, and it proved impossible to present a consumer pack such that the housewife could just defrost it and cook.

She and her sisters were costly to operate, more heavily manned than others. Their disadvantages were compensated by the volume of hauls in the comparatively underfished grounds of the North West Atlantic only until others, bigger and more ruthless, came to share the feast. When the state-subsidised Iron Curtain countries' fleets, free of economic restraint, arrived to denude the grounds with their carbon copies of *Fairtry* and latterly with more efficient progeny, such marginal profit as there was soon was dissipated.

The experiment might have been abandoned long before it was, as some senior members of the board advocated. In boardroom debates Max Harper Gow was criticised for involving the company in increasing expense of what others saw as a lossmaking undertaking. "But," he said later, "Captain Harold supported me because he was longsighted enough to think that it might lead to something, or that at least it could keep the company going."

As proved to be the case.

He was able to add a postscript to that previous disappointing message to the shareholders:

"Some consolation," he said, "must lie in the fact that the *Fairtrys* were responsible for your company securing its dominant position in the frozen food industry, which, though less exciting, has proved much more profitable."

CHAPTER THIRTEEN

Captain Harold Keith Salvesen, co-architect of the fishing revolution, died in an Edinburgh nursing home on 1st February, 1970, at the age of 72.

In his lifetime he had made many gifts to good causes, some in the family name and others anonymously, and characteristically he made no attempt to evade or to ameliorate the burden of death duties. Much of his estate of over £4 million went to the State. His widow Mora, eldest daughter of Admiral John Ewen Cameron, explained: "He did this for the good of the country. That was his idea about his money."

His friend, G. P. S. Macpherson, revealed that Captain Harold would have liked to incorporate the word 'ventures' into the name of the family firm because he thought it was characteristic of the business he had done so much to develop. When he registered his coat of arms he substituted his father's motto *Inveni Portum* (I Have Found a Harbour) with that of *Maris Aequor Rursus Arabo* (I Will Plough the Waters of the Deep Once More).

The waters had been ploughed well.

The group by then employed 2700 people—a thousand more than had gone with the expeditions in the latter days of whaling—and 300 seafarers.

The cold storage business, which Barry Sealey diversified into processing for themselves and for others, had 26 million cubic feet of cold storage in seven centres, a potato chip factory, two companies manufacturing equipment for the industry, and a transport company.

Gerald Elliot's fishing operations encompassed other fishmeal processing plants, in Canada and in Eire, and in the UK a canning factory, a large processing and merchanting company, and an inshore fishing and selling company.

The expansion made mockery of the old Dickensian offices in Leith; 29 to 37 Bernard Street's honeycomb of rooms so bulged that offices at the rear were used as warehouses, the overcrowding finally compelling them to build a new headquarters in grounds near Fettes College in the city.

Captain Harold had taken his company out of whaling with less distress for his shareholders and friends than might otherwise have been the case, and he had seen his young partners in whom he had placed his confidence go forward into a promising new business era.

But it had been at a cost.

It should be remembered he lived through an age in which attitudes to whaling were very different. Few regarded it as other than an acceptable commercial pursuit. (Who might imagine a government of the present urging housewives to include whalemeat in the family diet, as was done in 1947?)

If it also can be held his concern for the whale coincided with commercial interest, it is fair to consider that his efforts to halt over-exploitation began when conservationists were very thin on the ground, and that his efforts persisted through times whether of good or of poor return.

When the International Whaling Commission finally adopted his favoured policy of national quotas, it was done too late, and without the safeguards that could have made it work.

The ending, however much he knew always to be inevitable, was painful to him, bringing parting not only from a way of life but from so many he regarded as his comrades.

It is doubtful also if he ever became reconciled to the fact that the alternative to emerge from his fishing experiment had been the dull-seeming cold storage and frozen food business, for he never interested himself in it.

Max Harper Gow called him "a most remarkable man, of great vision."

But farsighted as he was, Captain Harold could not have envisaged his business as it is today.

The family still owns 40% of the equity, though it became a public company in 1985.

The traditional shipping business, which pre-dated whaling outlived it by another 26 years; Salvesen 'swallowed the anchor' with the sale of its last vessel in 1989.

Several paths taken by the partners after whaling were subsequently abandoned or diverged from along the way. The fishing interests, which under Gerald Elliot became a substantial presence in that industry, contracted as the industry itself did, and were disposed of while still making money. So too were the housebuilding companies, which had grown to take their place among the most important. The company also withdrew from the North Sea oil and gas industry in which its Oilfield Technology company had developed an important role—this, as with other disposals, in favour of concentration on other core activity. The last links with the manufacturing activities—the quality brickmaking company Salvesen Brick, and the Vikoma company which specialises in equipment for the control of offshore oil pollution—were loosening when these two businesses were put up for sale at the beginning of 1995. The successful completion of the sale of Brick in March 1995 gave far greater focus to the company's strategy of concentration of group resources on its international Distribution and Specialist Hire activities.

How radically the company has transformed was evidenced in 1992 when the Stock Exchange classifications changed to include a Business Services sector. Salvesen, as an international supplier of business services in 16 countries, is one of the largest concerns among those listed.

Its core activities include a business that belongs to the technological era that Captain Harold never knew. This is Specialist Hire, in which Aggreko is the world's leading mobile power and temperature control rental company, operating from depots in Europe, North America, the Middle East and the Asia Pacific region.

But the two other core divisions can be said to derive from the day in the 1950s when the Grimsby cold stores could not take in *Fairtry*'s fish.

The cold storage business became 'Food Services' after Barry Sealey began to process for others, and Food Services now not only processes for most of the leading manufacturers throughout the UK, but also packs, stores and delivers for them.

Distribution began with the delivery of frozen and chilled food to retail chains, and since then has grown as a division in itself, serving leading manufacturers and retailers in food, consumer and industrial sections of the logistics market throughout the UK, Continental Europe and the United States.

Two decades after Captain Harold's death, the company employs more than 11,000 people, and operates in some 20 countries around the world.

Contrastingly, no good fortune attended the latter years of the inventor whose creativeness initiated the fishing revolution.

There are few headlines to tell of Sir Dennis Burney during the 13 years that followed the formation of his fishing and research company with Sir Murray Stephen and the Hellyer brothers—which was where we left him in our story.

Bill Lochridge, on leaving *Fairtry* to rejoin him in 1955, had said, 'It was just like beginning again where we had stopped'.

Where they had stopped was in the midst of experiments with Sir Dennis' parotters, which lifted the net off the bottom and had given him hope of a solution of how to trawl at any depth.

The two friends resumed these experiments in the Hellyer side trawler *Benvolio*. She was rigged with her normal trawling gear on the port side so that the parotters could be used on the other, and Bill Lochridge designed an electronic device to give signals from the net to the depthfinder in the wheelhouse so that they would tell at any time where the net would be if a shoal was found. With this device, which they managed to make so cheaply that Bill Lochridge christened it 'Our Willie Woodbine Asdic', and with the parotters, they fished the northern grounds for the next three years.

Bill Lochridge left him to go to India in 1958. He had overstayed his contract with the research company by seven months, and, he said, "I thought the work was done. We caught almost as many fish on the bottom with the parotters as with the otter boards, but we did not catch many in midwater. Hellyer did not seem to think it was worthwhile to go on."

But for Sir Dennis there had been called a mere halt.

Meanwhile, he proposed to send orthodox trawlers on six-week expeditions to the Newfoundland Grand Banks, feeding a 'mother'. Unlike previous expeditions, 'mother' would not be a large ship but a cold store ashore in Bermuda, converted from the disused naval base. The trawlers would take their hauls there, just a few days steaming distance away, unload, fish the Banks again, return to the island and after discharging their second catch, reload with a cargo of frozen fish to take back to the home market.

In negotiations with executives of the island's legislative council he also proposed setting up a fishmeal processing factory.

By 1964 he was still hopeful his plans would go ahead, and he sold his country home and moved with his wife to the island. "But I wouldn't say I was going for good," he was reported as saying, and he commuted from Bermuda to renew midwater trawl experiments in the North Sea, for which he secured other backers in the shipping concern of Cayzer Irvine.

After two years in which misfortunes dogged the work, he was becoming despondent. He was 77, in indifferent health, though he insisted he had no thought of retiring. "*That* would be dull," he said.

As he prepared to go to sea on tests on board the 270 ton North Shields steam trawler *Relko*, he complained, "I've begun to think I must be plagued by gremlins," and he determined, "Unless we pull it off I'll pack it in." He fell ill and *Relko* sailed without him.

Lady Burney flew from Bermuda as he went into hospital for an emergency operation.

The patient was out of hospital and resting at his sister's home in London when *Relko* returned from tests 800 miles north of Aberdeen, and her skipper called him by telephone to tell him—"It's a winner."

The report was over-optimistic. Much remained to be done. His son Sir Cecil said: "Illness halted the work. Looking back on it now, I think he was ill from around 1963 or even 1962."

In December 1968, as *Fairtry* was passing out of British hands, *The Times* reported the death of Commander Sir Charles Dennistoun Burney, Bt., CMG, aged 79, at his home in Hamilton, Bermuda.

The obituary occupied 128 lines and recorded all his

achievements before and during World War I and into the 1930s. After that—nothing.

Throughout the 1950s and 1960s, the West German scientist Dr Joachim Scharfe was engaged along almost identical lines and his netsonde technique, or variants of it, came to be used all over the world. It is he who is credited with giving to the fishing industry the midwater trawl system which to the end of his days eluded Sir Dennis Burney.

The inventor died a frustrated man.

EPILOGUE

In the 1970s everyone accepted that the seas were overfished, but observance of restriction was accepted only so long as it applied to others.

The distance-no-object ships, with their improved navigational aids and sonar systems, swept the seas remorselessly for demersal fish from the Grand Banks to the coasts of Africa. The purse seine netters, whose capabilities had been transformed by the invention of a mechanical power block, took toll of the pelagics.

But Dr Joachim Scharfe's invention gave a new dimension to catching potential. With the midwater trawl the roving fleets could catch pelagic fish as well as demersals in volume comparable with that of the seine netters.

The march towards the 200 mile fishing limit gathered relentless pace, and the British distant water trawlermen who had dismissed it as an absurdity less than 20 years before became haunted by the fear of losing traditional grounds.

Just as the First Cod War of 1958 to 1961 had ended on Iceland's terms, so too did the second, when eleven years later, she extended from 12 to 50 miles (giving as one reason that "otherwise the Russians will come in"). In 1975 she stretched the limit to 200 miles, precipitating the Third Cod War. This was even more fiercely contested, with shots exchanged and with as many as 45 collisions between Icelandic gunboats and the frigates sent to protect the British trawlermen fishing inside their box formations.

When peace came in May 1976 some saw the agreement as the fishing industry's death warrant. The signatory was Anthony Crosland, UK Foreign and Commonwealth Affairs Minister, who, ironically, was MP for Grimsby. Friends said his death within a year, at the age of 59, had been hastened by the emotional turmoil he suffered.

107

His widow scattered his ashes in the Humber estuary, off the town whose interests he had served for 18 years.

The treaty was to run for just six months and was the last to be negotiated bilaterally between the two countries. During the six months Britain's presence in Iceland's 200 mile zone was restricted to no more than 24 trawlers in a day.

Within a year the nations along both sides of the North Atlantic, from the United States and Canada on the one to Britain and other EEC adherents on the other, and Norway and Russia, had accepted the 200 mile limit as received gospel. There was then 'No Entry Without Permission' all the way from the Barents Sea and the White Sea across to Newfoundland. Britain's bargaining rights were subsumed within the EEC, and in the events that followed that body did our fishermen few favours.

Several of the more efficient freezers continued nevertheless to make a reasonable living for some time. Others scattered as far as Australia and New Zealand; some became mother ships among foreign catching fleets; some were sold—cheaply—abroad, and an elite few were converted as hydrographic survey vessels.

For the sidetrawlers, however, apart from a score or more which acted for some years as standby safety vessels in the North Sea oilfields, there was suddenly nowhere to go.

Grimsby had a diversity of vessels to sustain it, but within a few years Hull harboured a graveyard of idle ships.

Could it have been different?

In the inevitable inquest there were many to accuse the trawler owners. Critics said they should have seen how the dice were loaded against them—100 countries supported the principle of the 200 mile limit at the Conference on the Law of the Sea, and a threat by Iceland to leave NATO had prompted strong political pressure from the Western allies who were alarmed by the prospective loss of their northern bastion. But instead of being prepared to compromise, the trawler owners gambled for higher stakes and paid the price.

Others said the owners had been too hidebound by tradition to march with the times, and to profit from the experience of *Fairtrys*. It is only fair to say in this regard that when the owners eventually accepted the principle of freezing at sea and followed the way charted for them by Torry this was correct for them, and that the stern trawling freezers which evolved, beginning with *Lord Nelson* and *Junella*, were the product of sound commercial judgment.

The charge that might be made more justly is that they were over-cautious, that they delayed too long to change; there was no protracted phase-in of the 200 mile limit, as some hoped there would be, in which they might have established a presence else-where and thus lent weight to negotiations for licences from other nations.

The reality is probably that whatever the trawler owners might have done, or failed to do, nothing would have altered the ultimate event. In those latter years the drama proceeded as inexorably as in a Greek tragedy.

As for the Russians, their world appeared to shrink at a stroke. They were shut out of some grounds altogether. They came to Britain—whose waters they had started to plunder—only as klondykers to buy our herring and our mackerel. Elsewhere they made such bargains for licences as they could.

Tony Hudson, returning from a visit to Murmansk, said: "I got a good look at the fleet in port there. It was enormous. All laid up because the Russians had become persona non grata almost every-where."

Yet within a decade of that time the Russians were catching 10 million metric tons a year. They exploited to the utmost their own coastal and inland waters and whichever other grounds that bar-gains permitted, but they looked also beyond the 200 mile limit to the vast deep waters, taking much of their catch from areas opened up by scientific exploration. Their supertrawlers have unlimited range, able to sustain themselves independently of the fleets' huge support trains, exchanging with one another where necessary their navigational fishfinding equipment, their spares, and even their engines.

The oceans of the world are now more intensively fished than ever before. Fishing ranges continuously in new areas—the capelin of the Arctic, the squid of the South Atlantic, the shrimp-like krill of the Antarctic, the food of Salvesen's whales. It is ironic that the overwhelming success of the fish factory ship is now helping to destroy the fish on which it thrived. We are now realising that our priority in fisheries is, not how to catch more efficiently, but how to limit harvesting of the world's fish stocks to ensure that they can renew themselves for the benefit of future generations.

The Salvesen family

HAROLD KEITH SALVESEN

Second son of Theodore, and grandson of the company founder Christian. Partner of Christian Salvesen and Co from 1930 until 1960. Director of The South Georgia Co Ltd from 1930 until 1967, (chairman from 1942 until 1964).

IVER

Cousin of Harold, son of Thomas and grandson of the founder. Partner from 1931 until his death in 1957. Director of The South Georgia Co Ltd during the same period. He had charge of the merchant fleet as had his father before him. His son Robin was appointed managing director of the marine division in 1969.

NOEL

Elder brother of Harold. Although he decided not to return to management after the war, he remained on the board of the parent company until 1963 when he retired at the age of 70.

NORMAN

Younger brother of Harold, last of the founder's four grandsons, died in 1978. Like Noel, did not return to management but remained a director of the parent company until retiring in 1972.

SIR (LEONARD) MAXWELL HARPER GOW, MBE

Great-grandson of the founder, Christian; grandson of Edward, Lord Salvesen, the Court of Session judge. Born in 1918, son of the late Leonard Harper Gow and Eleanor Amalie Salvesen. Awarded the MBE for war services in 1944. Partner of

Christian Salvesen and Co in 1947; director of the parent company, The South Georgia Co Ltd, in 1952; chairman and managing director of Christian Salvesen and Co Ltd (successors to the partnership) in 1960; chairman from 1964 (and its managing director until 1973) of The South Georgia Co Ltd which became Christian Salvesen Ltd after 1969; retired from chairmanship in 1981 and continued as non-executive vice chairman until 1987. Knighted in 1985.

SIR GERALD (HENRY) ELLIOT
Great-grandson of Christian; grandson of Theodore; nephew of Harold. Born in 1923, son of the late Surgeon Captain J. S. Elliot, RN, and Magda Salvesen. Partner of Christian Salvesen and Co in 1955; director of The South Georgia Co Ltd from 1957; director from 1960 of Christian Salvesen and Co Ltd, successors to the partnership; vice chairman and managing director in 1973 of Christian Salvesen Ltd, which had succeeded The South Georgia Co Ltd. He followed Sir Maxwell in the chair in 1981, and retired in 1988. Knighted in 1986.

Salvesen executives and staff

BARRY EDWARD SEALEY
Born 1936. BA (Hons) Cambridge; Harvard Business School 1968. Joined company in 1958, appointed managing director Christian Salvesen (Grimsby) Ltd 1965; managing director Food Services Division in 1969; managing director of the group 1981; deputy chairman and managing director 1987 until retirement from post in 1990. Awarded CBE in 1990 in recognition of services to industry.

EDWARD SEALEY
Father of Barry. Born 1909. Director of cold storage division which his son headed, and had charge of the operation in England until forced by illness to retire at end of 1971.

Remained as a non-executive director of the division until he was 65. He now lives in retirement in Edinburgh.

WILLIAM M. B. GREENFIELD
On landing at Leith Harbour base in 1945, deckboy Willie Greenfield was designated deckboy/assistant secretary. He was appointed assistant secretary of *Southern Venturer* in February, 1946. For the next ten years he divided his duties between the expeditions and head office, latterly as assistant to the manager of the crew department, until becoming secretary of *Southern Venturer* in 1956. He was recalled to head office in 1958, crewing the merchant ships and *Fairtrys*. Subsequently he managed Salvesen's fishmeal plant in Ireland, and then became manager of the company's cold store in Inverness. He returned to head office in 1988 as Scottish sales manager before retiring in 1990. He is secretary of the Ex-Whalers' Club, which meets regularly in Leith and at intervals in the Shetlands and in South Shields. The club has links also with Norwegian former whalers in Tønsberg and in Sandefjord.

WILLIAM F. LYNCH
On his return from Antarctica Bill Lynch became a purchasing clerk at head office. Five years later he was appointed as the group's purchasing superintendent, which post he held until his retirement in 1982. He lives with his family in Edinburgh.
During the Falklands war he was able to provide the Navy with detailed description and pictures and drawings of Grytviken and Leith Harbour. Admiral James Kennon, Chief of Fleet Support, in a letter of thanks said he appreciated the speed with which he had come to the aid of his Directorate of Administrative Planning and said his advice and information had made a valuable contribution. He is chairman of the Ex-Whalers' Club.

COMMANDER SIR CHARLES DENNISTOUN BURNEY
Born December 1888, eldest son of Admiral Sir Cecil Burney, 1st baronet, and of Lucinda Marion. Awarded CBE in 1917. MP for Uxbridge (Cons) from 1922 until 1929. Inventor of paravane, designer and builder of airship R100, author of *The World, the Air and the Future* (1929). Died, 1968.

WILLIAM LOCHRIDGE
Born 1911, educated at Airdrie Academy. Intended a career in architecture, but finding no opening turned to marine engineering. Trained as engineer and draughtsman at Wm Beardmore and Co Ltd, Glasgow, served several years afterwards at sea, mostly with Glen Line ships. Joined Sir Dennis Burney on arms development in 1941; manager of inventor's Broadway Trust and of Fresh Frozen Foods Ltd until Sir Dennis sold to Salvesen; continued then with the *Fairtry* venture in Salvesen company until 1956, and then rejoined Sir Dennis. In 1958 went to the P&O group's company Mazagon Dock Ltd in India, first as manager, then managing director. Returned to UK in 1961 as engineering manager of Alexander Stephen and Sons' shipyard and in 1968 joined a small UK management team which converted the naval dockyard at Singapore as one of the world's biggest commercial repair yards. 'Retired' in 1975, acted as self-employed marine consultant for eight more years before finally tiring of crawling amid machinery and double bottom tanks.

FRED SCHOFIELD
Remained with Salvesen as technical director of fishing operations. He died in 1986.

CAPTAIN JIM WHITE
Sailed with *Fairtry* originally as mate, then became her factory manager. He died in retirement in 1978.

J. CARL ROSS
He resigned the chairmanship of his group in 1968—one year before the Imperial takeover—following reported board-room disputes, and was succeeded by Sir Alex Alexander. He then continued in business till his death in 1986, channelling most of his energies into Cosalt (the Grimsby Coal Salt and Tanning Company), described as 'the piscatorial Harrod's' because for a century it supplied the fishing industry with whatever it needed.

JOHN BENNETT
He was managing director of Associated Fisheries after his father's death; the title was abolished in 1966 when he became deputy chairman. He held that post until he retired 20 years later, remaining a director of the company. He had to fight off three attempts by Carl Ross to take over the business his father formed. The last bid was blocked by the Monopolies Commission in 1966. But three years later the Government's Industrial Reorganisation Corporation fathered a merger of a different kind; the deep sea fleets were hived off from the interests of both groups to form British United Trawlers under an independent chairman. Of the 120 vessels united by the forced marriage, none of the sidewinders survived after 1975 in the industry, and by 1986 the last of the stern trawling freezers went to foreign owners.

LEOPOLD DIXON ROMYN
Born 1902 at Burgess Hill, Sussex, son of John Richard Dixon Romyn and Mabel Eleanor, daughter of Admiral Selwyn. Educated at Lancing College Sussex. Joined shipbroking firm of Brown and Atkinson in Hull and stayed three years before signing on a Hull trawler. Married Gudrun Alette Anthi, probationary nurse whom he met when he broke a leg on a fishing trip and was taken to hospital in Vardo, Norway. Joined RNVR at outbreak of war, and served as Skipper

Lieutenant throughout, afterwards joining J Marr and Son as trawler skipper until joining Salvesen in 1954. After leaving *Fairtrys* in 1962 spent three years with Marr then rejoined Salvesen, surveying fisheries for the company in areas off South Arabia, the east coast of Canada and Denmark. He died in 1976. Max Harper Gow said of him: "He saved the experiment from disaster. If we had not secured a first class skipper for *Fairtry* and if he had not stayed to train up others I doubt if the experiment would have lasted long."

LOFTUR JULIUSSON
Remained with the *Fairtrys* until 1965, sailing to distant grounds, was duly promoted and left only after a spell of illness. His service record described him as "a very reliable and conscientious man."

The Torry scientists

DR. GEORGE ADAM REAY
Native of Aberdeen, educated at the university there and at Cambridge. He joined the Department of Scientific and Industrial Research in 1929 and was posted immediately to the newly-forming Torry Research Station. He devoted his entire working career to investigation into the preservation of fish. In 1937 he succeeded Dr Adrian Lumley as the station's superintendent (the title was changed to that of director in 1958). He was awarded the OBE in 1949, and the CBE in 1958. When he retired in 1964 the station which had begun with a staff of five had as many as 200 people at work there. Dr Reay died in 1971, aged 69.

DR. GORDON EDDIE
Gordon Eddie headed Torry engineering department from 1946 to 1962. When the White Fish Authority, forerunner of the present day Sea Fish Industry Authority, established its Industrial Development Unit in Hull, he was appointed the

Authority's technical director, and later its deputy chief executive. He made many valuable contributions to the fishing industry in the fields of fish handling, processing, preservation and distribution, and helped in the formation of the Fisheries and Offshore Oil Consultative Group, aimed at solving conflicts of interest between fishermen and oilmen. Dr Eddie was fisheries member of Lord Shackleton's inquiry into the future of the Falkland Islands, South Georgia and British interests in the Antarctic, and he also contributed to a further report in 1982. He died at home in Deeside in 1991.

The frozen food pioneers

SIR ALEX SANDOR ALEXANDER

Son of a Czech wine grower, he was finishing medical studies when the Nazis closed Prague University. He came to England as a refugee and took a post as tutor to the son of a fruit farmer in Westwick. In 1947 he started a freezing company in which Carl Ross took half the shares. Five years later Carl Ross took over his interests and brought him with them into his group. In 1954 he joined the Ross parent board, and rose rapidly in that organisation. He succeeded Carl Ross as chairman in 1968. When the company was absorbed by Imperial he became chairman of Ross Smedley and then had, under one umbrella, Ross, Smedley, HP Sauce, and Golden Wonder Chips. Two years later, in 1971, he became chairman of Imperial. He was knighted in 1971. Sir Alex retired from Imperial chairmanship in 1979, but then chaired J Lyons and Co till 1989.

A. H. (MICK) COBURN, CBE

Mick Coburn spent a lifetime in the frozen food business, in which he became a legendary figure and affectionately known as the Codfather. At a time when fish sent by road went in lorries covered by tarpaulin, he sent the first insulated lorry out of Grimsby. He and his Scots engineering friend Alex

117

Stephens took a container such as was used for furniture removals bound for abroad, nailed it all round inside with a cork lining eight inches deep and hoisted the box on a lorry. The Eskimo business, which Bill Bennett gave him and Joe Sprott to expand as a challenge to Birds Eye, itself became later a three-company amalgam, and was then absorbed by Findus with Mick Coburn heading it until his retirement.

MARGARET SWALLOW
Margaret Swallow retired from Smethurst's in 1965 and died seven years later.

LOUISE GIBB
After Smethurst was merged into Birds Eye she was transferred to Kirby as manager there. For her, the wheel had turned full circle; she had begun her career with Unilever as the first woman in their Port Sunlight laboratory. She died in retirement in 1989.

MRS LILLIAN WELLS
Lillian Wells was among the first to freeze peas and other vegetables after the war, marketing them from her cold store as 'Winter Sunshine'. "And believe it or not, we blanched the peas in domestic copper boilers," she said, "and we timed them with egg timers." When others had no freezers she installed twelve of Carl Ross' Jackstone frosters at the cold store for those who could not afford to buy. Mrs Wells died in 1990.